PRACTICAL ADVICE ON SECTION 504 FOR EDUCATORS

First Printing: 2018

ISBN 978-0-578-21092-6

Booth Law Group LLC (763) 253-4155
www.boothlawgroup.com

TABLE OF CONTENTS

DISCLAIMER

This document was not created to render formal legal advice. While we have made our best effort to ensure accurate information, this document is not legal advice. Please contact your attorney regarding specific questions as each situation presents unique facts that must be considered before advice may be rendered.

OVERVIEW OF SECTION 504 OF THE REHABILITATION ACT OF 1973 AND RELATED STATUTES

Section 504 Prohibits Discrimination

"No otherwise qualified individual with a disability . . . shall, solely by reason of her or his disability, be excluded from the participation in, be denied the benefits of, or be subjected to discrimination under any program or activity receiving Federal financial assistance."

29 U.S.C. § 794(a) ("Section 504").

Section 504: Disability Discrimination

Section 504 of the Rehabilitation Act of 1973 prohibits discrimination against individuals with disabilities by entities including public schools receiving federal financial assistance. Our focus is on students with disabilities within the educational setting. We address disability discrimination in employment briefly at the end of this manual.

The Federal Statute

Section 504 of the Rehabilitation Act of 1973, as amended, provides that "no otherwise qualified individual with a disability . . . shall, solely by reason of her or his disability, be excluded from the participation in, be denied the benefits of, or be subjected to discrimination under any program or activity receiving Federal financial assistance." 29 U.S.C. § 794(a). The term "program or activity" is defined to include school districts. 29 U.S.C. § 794(b)(2)(B).

The Federal Regulations

The federal regulations under Section 504 are set forth at 34 C.F.R. § 104.

Purpose

The purpose of the federal regulations is to effectuate Section 504 of the Rehabilitation Act of 1973, "which is designed to eliminate discrimination on the basis of handicap in any program or activity receiving Federal financial assistance." 34 C.F.R. § 104.1.

Discrimination Prohibited

School districts (and other recipients of federal funding) may not, directly or through contractual, licensing, or other arrangements, on the basis of disability:

1. Deny a qualified disabled person the opportunity to participate in or benefit from the aid, benefit, or service;

2. Afford a qualified disabled person an opportunity to participate in or benefit from the aid, benefit, or service that is not equal to that afforded others;

3. Provide a qualified disabled person with an aid, benefit, or service that is not as effective as that provided to others;

4. Provide different or separate aid, benefits, or services to disabled persons or to any class of disabled persons unless such action is necessary to provide qualified disabled persons with aid, benefits, or services that are as effective as those provided to others;

5. Aid or perpetuate discrimination against a qualified disabled person by providing significant assistance to an agency, organization, or person that discriminates on the basis of disability in providing any aid, benefit, or service to beneficiaries of the recipients program or activity;

6. Deny a qualified disabled person the opportunity to participate as a member of planning or advisory boards; or

7. Otherwise limit a qualified disabled person in the enjoyment of any right, privilege, advantage, or opportunity enjoyed by others receiving an aid, benefit, or service. 34 C.F.R. § 104.4.

Disability Defined

The term "handicapped person" means:

1. A physical or mental impairment that substantially limits one or more major life activities;

2. A record of such impairment; or

3. Being regarded as having such an impairment. 34 C.F.R. § 104.3(j).

This definition is somewhat different than the way we use the term "handicapped" in common speech. Disability is defined by Section 504 to prevent discrimination against a person who has a physical or mental impairment that is one who we would in common language the term "handicapped." The statute also protects from discrimination two categories of persons who do not have a physical or mental condition that in common language would term them as handicapped. The law's purpose is to prevent discrimination against those who previously were handicapped (have a record of impairment) or those who are not handicapped, but are treated as if they were handicapped (are regarded as handicapped). The school district may not discriminate against these two groups of people by, for example, prohibiting the student who had situational depression but no longer has depression from playing a sport.

It is important to note that while Section 504 protects all three categories from discrimination, only the student who has an actual physical or mental condition is eligible for a 504 Plan. Schools do not provide a 504 Plan to a student who is regarded as disabled but is not; nor do schools provide a 504 Plan for a student who used to be disabled but is no longer a person with a physical or mental condition.

Comparing Section 504, the ADA, and IDEA

Anti-Discrimination Statutes Versus Funding Statute

As stated above, **Section 504** prohibits discrimination on the basis of disability in programs or activities that receive financial assistance from the federal government, e.g., school districts which receive federal funds through the U.S. Department of Education. Title II of the **Americans with Disabilities Act** of 1990 (Title II) extends this prohibition against discrimination to all state and local government agencies and programs (including public schools) regardless of whether they receive federal financial assistance.

The **Individuals with Disabilities Education Act (IDEA)** is the federal statute which funds special education programs. In order to receive federal funding, states must take steps to ensure that local school districts are meeting the IDEA's many requirements. In contrast, Section 504 and the ADA are anti-discrimination statutes and do not provide any type of funding.

The Office for Civil Rights, a component of the U.S. Department of Education, enforces Section 504 and the ADA as applied to schools. The Office of Special Education and Rehabilitative Services (OSERS), also a component of the U.S. Department of Education, administers the Individuals with Disabilities Education Act.

Section 504 Provides More Coverage Than IDEA

Section 504 requires that students with disabilities be provided with a free appropriate public education (FAPE). The regulations require identification, evaluation, provision of appropriate accommodations, and procedural safeguards in every public school in the United States. These requirements are similar to, though generally less procedurally complex, than the requirements under the IDEA.

Section 504 covers a broader range of students than the IDEA. This is because Section 504 protects students that meet the broad definition of "disabled," while the IDEA requires special education and related services only for those students that meet specific criteria for certain enumerated disabling conditions which affect learning.

Generally, any student who qualifies for special education under the IDEA will also meet the definition of disabled under Section 504. In contrast, not all students who have been determined to be disabled under Section 504 will meet the criterion for coverage under the IDEA. The diagram below is illustrative of this distribution of students.

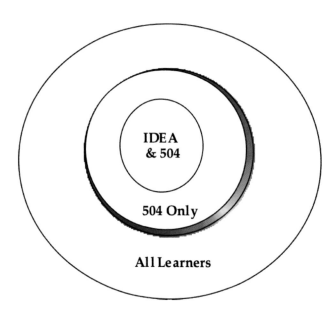

The 2008 ADA Amendments

On January 1, 2009, the Americans with Disabilities Act Amendments Act of 2008 ("ADAAA") went into effect. These Amendments were incorporated into Section 504.

A Shift from Whether to What

The Amendments shifted the focus of ADA and Section 504 compliance from the question of whether a person's impairment is a disability, to the interactive process through which the school and parents (or employer/employee) determine what is necessary to reasonably accommodate the disability. In this vein Congress stated that "the question of whether an individual's impairment is a disability under the [Act] should not demand extensive analysis."

Broadening the Class of Protected Persons

The ADAAA did not change the definition of "disability." However, Congress expressly rejected two major Supreme Court decisions that Congress believed improperly restricted the definition of "disability" and narrowed the class of persons protected by the ADA.

Congress Rejects two Supreme Court Cases

In *Sutton et al. v. United Air Lines, Inc.*, 527 U.S. 471 (1999), the Supreme Court held that the determination of whether a person was disabled had to be made after taking into account the ameliorative effects of mitigation measures, such as medication or medical devices. The ADAAA explicitly prohibits the consideration of "mitigating measures" in determining whether an individual qualifies as "disabled." Now the determination must be made "without regard to the ameliorative effects of mitigating measures" such as medication, medical supplies, prosthetics, hearing aids, mobility devices, assistive technology and learned behavior or neurological modifications. However, contact lenses and eyeglasses may be taken into account in determining whether an individual qualifies as "disabled."

Thus, for example, an individual with diabetes may be found to have a disability under the law, even if when taking medication, he has no symptoms. Note that while this change may broaden the class of students covered, in some cases it may not actually change the service/accommodations a school would need to provide. For example, a student who can function at a high level despite learning disabilities, because of his or her own adaptations (learned behavior or neurological modifications), may not require an accommodation for his or her disability.

In *Toyota Motor Mfg., Kentucky, Inc. v. Williams*, 534 U.S. 184 (2002), the Supreme Court held that the terms "substantially limited" and "major life activities" should be read <u>narrowly</u> and that an individual must show that a disability prevents or "severely restricts" him from doing activities that are of central importance to most people's lives. In the ADAAA Congress rejected the severely restricted standard as too high and stated that [t]he definition of disability shall be construed in favor of broad coverage of individuals under this Act, to the maximum extent permitted by the terms of this Act. Beyond rejecting the severely restricted standard and instructing courts and agencies to favor broad coverage, the Supreme Court did not set out what it means for an individual to have a physical or mental impairment that "substantially limits" a major life activity. Those determinations will need to be made on a case by case basis keeping in mind Congress's instruction to favor broad coverage.

Congress' Guidance in the ADAAA

In addition to rejecting these Supreme Court decisions, Congress provided guidance for determining whether an individual's impairment is considered a disability. Most significantly, Congress:

1. Emphasized that the definition of "disability" should be interpreted broadly;

2. Directed the Equal Employment Opportunity Commission ("EEOC") to revise/broaden the portion of its regulations defining the term "substantially limits";

3. Defined "major life activities" by including two non-exhaustive lists:

    a) "Major life activities" include, but are not limited to: "caring for oneself, performing manual tasks, seeing, hearing, eating, sleeping, walking, standing, lifting, bending,

12

speaking, breathing, learning, reading, concentrating, thinking, communicating and working;"

b) Note that reading, thinking, concentrating, and communicating were not formerly in the Section 504 regulations;

c) "Major life activities" also includes "major bodily functions," including, but not limited to "functions of the immune system, normal cell growth, digestive, bowel, bladder, neurological, brain, respiratory, circulatory, endocrine, and reproductive functions";

d) Clarified that an impairment that substantially limits one major life activity need not limit other major life activities in order to be a disability;

e) Clarified that an impairment that is episodic (defined as 6 months or less) or in remission is a disability if it would substantially limit a major life activity <u>when active</u>.

<u>Trending Toward Broader Coverage</u>

Even before the 2008 Amendments, things had been trending toward broader ADA and Section 504 coverage for students. For example, in January of 2007, the Office for Civil Rights ("OCR") questioned a school district's determination that a student with a peanut allergy was ineligible for a Section 504 Plan. The OCR found that given the severity of the student's peanut allergy (which included potential anaphylaxis according to his doctor) and given "the likelihood, nature, and severity of the harm that could result from the school district's failure to find the student eligible for Section 504 services," the school district likely violated Section 504 and the ADA by refusing to develop a plan for the student. The district subsequently entered into a Voluntary Agreement with the OCR. Similarly, even before the ADA Amendments, some schools had begun developing Section 504 plans for students with celiac disease.

<u>In Many Ways, the ADA is the Same as Before</u>

Although the ADAAA made some significant changes, the ADA Amendments retain the ADA's basic definition of "disability." And while coverage may be broader, the Section 504 process remains the same. The determination of whether a student qualifies for a 504 Plan and what that plan looks like has always been, and will remain, highly individual and must be made on a case by case basis.

<u>ADA Amendments' Effect on Section 504 Regulations</u>

The ADA Amendments Act required the EEOC to revise its regulations and the EEOC published its revised regulations in late 2010. Although the ADA Amendments Act also amended Section 504, Congress did not require the U.S. Department of Education to revise its Section 504 regulations and the Education Department has not done so. However, the OCR has stated it will enforce the current Section 504 regulations consistent with the Amendments Act. As such, we have noted ADA Amendments Act changes where appropriate in these materials.

From Process to Outcome

<u>Due Process- Notice and an Opportunity to be Heard</u>

A critical component of Section 504 is the due process afforded to parents, guardians and students.[1] Parents are entitled to due process in the form of notice of their rights and notice as to what the school district proposes. Parents are also entitled to an opportunity to be heard and to participate in the education plan for their child.

<u>Outcome</u>

When the Office for Civil Rights ("OCR") investigates a claim under Section 504 it is first concerned with whether the school district has followed a lawful process of identifying and evaluating a student suspected of having a disability. This process is referred to as "child-find." The OCR generally does not question a team's decision about eligibility or what should be in a student's 504 Plan. In recent years, OCR appears to be more focused on the outcome of the school district's 504 process; that is, did the district recognize the disability and if the student was found eligible for a plan, is the plan being implemented and producing results for the students.

---

[1] For the remainder of the guide, "parent(s)" includes guardians and students over 18 years old.

14

Section 504 is an anti-discrimination statute and its purpose is to ensure that students with disabilities have access that is similar to their peers. A 504 Plan is one way that a school district can ensure access and prevent discrimination.

Q&A: Section 504 Basics

1. Who is eligible for a 504 Plan?

   A. Only students who have a physical or mental impairment that substantially limits a major life activity are eligible for a 504 Plan.

2. Is a student who has a history of impairment eligible for a 504 Plan?

   A. **No.** Students who do not have a present impairment are not entitled to a 504 Plan. For example, a student **is not eligible for a 504 Plan** under these facts. The student had melanoma (a form of skin cancer), and the cancer was surgically removed, leaving the student cancer free. The student does not have a present physical or mental impairment, so he or she is not eligible for a 504 Plan. The student cannot be discriminated against under Section 504 based on his or her history of once having cancer.

   In most cases, schools will have a medical or mental health diagnosis to document that a disability truly exists. In the few cases where a diagnosis is not possible, seek advice from a 504 coordinator or an attorney.

3. Is a student who is regarded as disabled, but who does not in fact have a disability, entitled to a 504 plan?

   A. **No.** For example, school staff often say that a student who appears to have ADHD is "regarded as having a disability," but **this is incorrect**. Unless there is an evaluation by the 504 Team, and (most times) medical documentation of ADHD, the school may not treat the student as disabled. In this example, it may be discriminatory to provide the student with a modified work schedule because she does not keep materials well organized and consequently does not complete work on time without objective evidence of a disability.

4. If a student has a 504 plan, is she automatically eligible for special education under IDEA?

   A. **No.** Section 504 is broader than the IDEA, and Section 504 covers more students than the IDEA. Just because an individual has a 504 plan does not mean she is eligible for IDEA services. On the other hand, generally all individuals who are eligible for IDEA services are also eligible for services under Section 504.

5. Do the ADA Amendments of 2008 affect Section 504?

   A. **Yes.** The ADA Amendments were incorporated into Section 504. Most notably, the amendments broadened the term "disability," allowing more individuals coverage under both the ADA and Section 504.

   Section 504 is broader than the IDEA. More students will be eligible for coverage under Section 504 than under the IDEA.

INDIVIDUAL WITH A DISABILITY

Photo by Joseph Allen
Washington D.C.

An "Individual with a Disability" is Protected

<u>Definition of Individual with a Disability</u>

Section 504 protects three classes of individuals. The statute covers individuals who have an **actual** disability, individuals who have a **record** of a disability, and individuals who are **regarded as** having a disability. More specifically, the federal regulations define an individual with a disability as any person who:

1. Has a physical or mental impairment which substantially limits one or more major life activities;

2. Has a record of such an impairment; or

3. Is regarded as having such an impairment. 34 C.F.R. § 104.3(j)(1).

<u>What is a Physical or Mental Impairment?</u>

Pursuant to 34 C.F.R. § 104.3(j)(2)(i) a **physical** impairment means: (1) any physiological disorder or condition; (2) cosmetic disfigurement; or (3) anatomical loss affecting one or more of the following body systems:

1. Neurological;

2. Musculoskeletal;

3. Special sense organs;

4. Respiratory (including speech organs);

5. Cardiovascular;

6. Reproductive;

7. Digestive;

8. Genital-urinary;

9. Hemic and lymphatic;

10. Skin; and

11. Endocrine.

A **mental** impairment means any mental or psychological disorder, such as: (1) intellectual disability; (2) organic brain syndrome; (3) emotional or mental illness; or (4) specific learning disabilities. 34 C.F.R. § 104.3(j)(2)(i).

What Does Substantially Limits Mean?

Neither the Section 504 regulations nor the ADA Amendments define the term "substantially limits." Exactly what that term means is an open question. However, school teams making Section 504 determinations should keep in mind that Congress intends the term to be interpreted broadly. Generally, the student's ability to perform a major life activity should be compared to peers, often using a common-sense analysis without scientific or medical advice.

Mitigating Measures

School teams must also remember that in a post-ADA Amendments world, whether an impairment "substantially limits" a major life activity must be determined without regard to the ameliorative effects of "mitigating measures." Pursuant to 42 U.S.C. § 12102(4)(E), **mitigating measures** include:

1. Medication;

2. Medical supplies or equipment including, but not limited to:

   a) Prosthetics such as limbs and devices;

   b) Hearing aids, cochlear implants, and other implantable hearing devices;

   c) Mobility devices;

   d) Oxygen therapy equipment and supplies; and

   e) Low-vision devices;

3. Assistive technology;

4. Reasonable accommodations;

5. Auxiliary aids or services, including:

   a) Qualified interpreters or other effective methods of making orally delivered materials available to individuals with hearing impairments; and

b) Qualified readers, taped texts, or other effective methods of making visually delivered materials available to individuals with visual impairments; or

6. Learned behavioral or adaptive neurological modifications.

Ordinary eyeglasses or contact lenses are **expressly excluded** from the list of mitigating measures. In other words, the ameliorating effects of eyeglasses and contact lenses are to be considered when determining whether an impairment substantially limits a major life activity.

What is a Major Life Activity?

Pre-ADA Amendments: Narrowly Construed	Post-ADA Amendments: Expanded View	Post-ADA Amendments: Inclusion of Major Bodily Functions
<ul><li>Caring for oneself</li><li>Performing manual tasks</li><li>Walking</li><li>Seeing</li><li>Hearing</li><li>Speaking</li><li>Breathing</li><li>Learning</li><li>Working</li></ul> 34 C.F.R. §104.3(j)(2)(ii)	<ul><li>Eating</li><li>Sleeping</li><li>Walking</li><li>Standing</li><li>Lifting</li><li>Bending</li><li>Reading</li><li>Concentrating</li><li>Thinking</li><li>Communicating</li></ul>	<ul><li>Functions of the immune system</li><li>Normal cell growth</li><li>Bowel Functions</li><li>Neurological functions</li><li>Brain functions</li><li>Circulatory functions</li></ul>

Before the ADA Amendments Act of 2008, courts often narrowly defined who was disabled. The ADA Amendments Act of 2008 expanded the definition of major life activity greatly. The Amendments added the functions seen in the middle column of the chart above, and the Amendments also included major bodily functions as a part of major life activity (as seen in the far right column of the chart above).

The inclusion of thinking, concentrating, and communicating in the non-exhaustive list of major life activities will undoubtedly raise difficult questions for school teams determining Section 504 eligibility. If a student is learning satisfactorily, but has substantial difficulty concentrating, is that student now entitled to a Section 504 Plan? In light of the ADA Amendments, such a student would appear to meet the definition of disabled. This is particularly true because in a post-ADA Amendments world, the school team must look at the child as he functions without "mitigating measures," which include medication. Thus, even if a student's ADHD is adequately controlled by medication, the student may still qualify as disabled under Section 504. However, qualifying as "disabled" would not end the inquiry. Instead, the inquiry will require a determination of whether the child's trouble concentrating results in the need for special education and related services. This is because the 504 regulations still include an educational need component. 34 C.F.R. §§ 104.33(b) and 104.35(a).

The inclusion of immune system functions on the list of "major bodily functions" has led to Section 504 protection for some students with food allergies, particularly if those allergies include life threatening anaphylaxis. Additionally, the inclusion of major bodily functions itself has led to "predictable" disabilities, such as cancer and diabetes.

<u>Who is a Qualified Student with a Disability?</u>

With respect to public preschool, elementary, secondary, or adult educational services, a learner is covered by Section 504 if the learner is: (1) of an age during which nondisabled learners are provided such services; (2) of any age during which it is mandatory under state law to provide such services to disabled learners; or (3) a student to whom the state is required to provide a free appropriate public education under the IDEA. 34 C.F.R. § 104.3(l)(2).

<u>What Does "Record of Impairment" and "Regarded as Having an Impairment" Mean?</u>

A student may also qualify for protection under Section 504 if the student has "a record of such impairment" or is "regarded as having such an impairment." 34 C.F.R. § 104.3(j)(1). It is important to note that although a student may qualify as "disabled" under these definitions and thus be entitled to protection from discrimination, that student is not guaranteed a 504 Plan.

Eligibility Determination

<u>Child Find Obligation</u>

The school district must evaluate any student who is believed to need special education or related services because of a disability. 34 C.F.R. § 104.35. Generally, referrals or requests for 504 evaluations will come from a parent, but anyone concerned about the need for a 504 evaluation, including teachers, school social workers, school nurses, school psychologists, and other educational staff can suggest the need for an evaluation.

Red Flags that may Suggest the Need to Consider a Section 504 Evaluation

- When suspension or expulsion is being considered for any learner.

- When retention is being considered or parent is requesting retention.

- When a learner shows a pattern of not benefiting from teacher instruction.

- When a learner returns to school after a serious illness or injury.

- When a learner is referred for evaluation, but it is determined not to do an evaluation under IDEA.

- When a learner is evaluated and found not to qualify for special education services under IDEA.

- When a learner has a chronic health condition even if it is episodic in nature or well cared for by an Individual Health Plan or by the student without adult intervention.

- When a learner has been identified as having an attention deficit disorder (ADD) or attention deficit hyperactive disorder (ADHD).

- When a learner is identified as "at risk" or exhibits the potential for dropping out of school.

- When a learner experiences a concussion.

- When substance abuse is an issue.

- When a disability of any kind is known or suspected.

- When a new building or remodeling is being considered (accessibility).

Evaluation Committee

Unlike the IDEA, Section 504 does not identify the persons (e.g. classroom teacher) required to be present when 504 decisions are made. The 504 regulations simply require that eligibility determinations be made by a group of persons knowledgeable about the child, the meaning of the evaluation data, and the placement options. 34 C.F.R. § 104.35(c)(3). Generally, the group would include the parent and several staff members from the student's building. If the parent does not agree with the school district's determination, the parent has a right to request a hearing on the matter. 34 C.F.R. § 104.36.

Evaluation Data

Formal tests are not required in a 504 determination. However, when formal tests are used, the tests must be selected and administered so as best to ensure that the test results accurately reflect the student's aptitude or achievement level or whatever other factor the test purports to measure, rather than reflecting the student's impaired sensory, manual, or speaking skills (except where those skills are the factors that the test purports to measure). In interpreting evaluation data and in making placement decisions, the school district must: (1) draw upon information from a variety of sources, including aptitude and achievement tests, teacher recommendations, physical condition, social or cultural background, and adaptive behavior, and (2) ensure that information obtained from all such sources is documented and carefully considered. 34 C.F.R. § 104.35(b).

When considering the "total student," one must rely on as much objective data as possible, including:

1. **Attendance Data** – is the disability impacting the student's ability to come to school or stay in school for the entire day? Do absences impact the student's academics, social and emotional learning or ability to participate in school in a way that is similar to their peers? Keep in mind that even if the student is receiving passing grades, lack of attendance can impact the student's ability to enjoy benefits of school that his or her peers enjoy.

2. **Behavior Data** – in-school suspensions, out-of-school suspensions, referrals, and behavioral tracking. Additionally, does the disability impact the student's ability to work in groups with peers on academic tasks? Does the student have decent relationships with adult educators? Do the relationships (or lack thereof) with others impact the student's ability to access education? Is the student's mental health condition impacting the student's ability to have access to the same activities as her peers?

3. **Academic Data** – Is the student making progress on standardized tests? Moving from grade to grade? Getting mostly passing grades? Making progress toward graduation? Given the student's abilities, what progress should be expected in the general education curriculum?

Timely Evaluation and Re-Evaluation as Necessary

The school is required to evaluate the student timely. Most schools have a policy or procedure that sets out the time limit for evaluation. It is acceptable, ***although not required***, to evaluate in 30 school days and re-evaluate every three years as is done under the Individuals with Disabilities Education Act (IDEA). Re-evaluation is only required by the law when the student needs re-evaluation or the parent or another team member requests re-evaluation.

Outside Data: Medical Diagnosis, Independent Evaluations

While it is advisable to request that the parent share a medical diagnosis with the school district if one exists, a school district cannot legally require a parent to obtain or provide a medical diagnosis regarding

24

the child's condition. If a parent does provide a physician's diagnosis, the school district should accept the medical/mental health diagnosis as true unless there is a strong reason to challenge it. (Seek legal advice if you decide to challenge the disability). Also, remember that if the parent provides a medical diagnosis, the school district may not rely exclusively on that medical diagnosis in making decisions regarding the child. The regulations require the school district to consider a variety of sources and consider the total student.

When a parent provides an independent evaluation, the school district similarly cannot (and need not) base its decisions solely on that evaluation. Instead, the evaluation should be considered alongside other sources of information about the child and should be accorded the weight it is due in light of all circumstances.

<u>Do any Physical or Mental Impairments Result in Automatic Qualification?</u>

Short Answer: No

Sometimes the question arises whether a particular injury, condition or diagnosis automatically qualifies a student under Section 504. The short answer is "no." This is because, the regulations do not contain any such list of qualifying conditions, and instead require that decisions about eligibility and services or adaptations must be made on a case by case basis. That being said, some severely disabling conditions will almost always result in a student being covered by Section 504.

The EEOC regulations do list a number of impairments that consistently will meet the definition of "disability." These include: deafness, blindness, intellectual disability, partially or completely missing limbs, mobility impairments requiring the use of a wheelchair, autism, cancer, cerebral palsy, diabetes, epilepsy, HIV/AIDS, multiple sclerosis, muscular dystrophy, major depression, bipolar disorder, post-traumatic stress disorder, obsessive-compulsive disorder, and schizophrenia.

<u>Does a School District have any obligations under Section 504 if a Parent refuses IDEA services?</u>

Pursuant to 34 C.F.R. §§ 300.9 and 300.300(b)(4), a parent may revoke consent in writing for all special education services at any time after the initial consent. Under the current state of the law, if a parent revokes consent under the IDEA or refuses initial services, the district should consider:

1. Whether the student may be eligible under Section 504 by completing a 504 evaluation; and

2. What program changes the student may need to prevent discrimination by the school based on her disability.

This has evolved over time. Recently, courts have concluded the revocation of consent under the IDEA does not eliminate the broader protection for students with disabilities under Section 504 and the ADA. *Kimble v. Douglas Cty. Sch. Dist. RE-1*, 925 F.Supp.2d 1176 (2013). "Section 504 permits Defendant to offer any other educational modifications or accommodations not encompassed by the IDEA's definitions of those services in order to meet its obligation to provide a FAPE." *Id.* at 1185. "[U]nlike FAPE under the IDEA, FAPE under Section 504 is defined to require a comparison between the manner in which the needs of disabled and non-disabled children are met and focuses on the 'design' of a child's educational program." *Jason E. ex rel. Linda E. v. Dep't of Educ.*, No. 12–00354, 2014 WL 6609213 (D. Haw., Nov. 20, 2014) (internal quotation omitted).

Special Issues

<u>Drug and Alcohol Use and Related Conditions</u>

Active illegal drug and alcohol use are treated differently under Section 504. A student actively engaging in the use of illegal drugs is not covered by Section 504, while a student actively using alcohol is covered by Section 504. However, the student in either case can be subjected to the school's normal disciplinary rules. *Halpern v. Wake Forest University Health Sciences*, 669 F.3d 454 (2012).

<u>Alcohol Use</u>

A student with a diagnosis of alcoholism, is a person with a disability. The 504 Team's evaluation of the student will determine if he or she requires program changes (accommodations or other services) in order to prevent discrimination. Regardless, the student is expected to follow state laws and school district policy prohibiting the use of alcohol. The student can be disciplined for alcohol use, possession or sale according to the district wide discipline policy (and the Minnesota High School League Rules, or state or local law).

<u>Successful Completion of a Drug Rehabilitation Program</u>

A student is considered to be a person with a disability and is protected from discrimination under Section 504. 42 U.S.C. § 12210(b) if the student: (1) successfully completes drug rehabilitation and is no longer engaging in the illegal use of drugs; (2) is participating in a supervised rehabilitation program and is no longer engaging in such use; or (3) is erroneously regarded as engaging in such use but is not using illegal drugs. The 504 Team would still need to evaluate the student, find the student eligible for 504 protections and then determine if program changes are required to prevent discrimination. For example, the student in recovery may need to leave school early to attend an aftercare program. The 504 Plan would excuse those absences.

__CAUTION__ - Keep in mind that a student who is using alcohol or drugs may have an underlying condition such as depression or anxiety that would qualify the student as disabled under Section 504 and the student may require a 504 Plan to prevent discrimination.

Temporary and Episodic Conditions

Under the ADA Amendments, an impairment that is episodic or in remission is still considered a disability if it would substantially limit a major life activity when active. Similarly, an impairment that is transitory or minor may qualify an individual as "regarded as being disabled" if the transitory impairment has an actual or expected duration of longer than 6 months.

Q&A: Individual with a Disability

1. Must schools re-evaluate students on a 504 Plan every year?

    A. **No**. Re-evaluation does not need to happen once per year nor does it have to happen at any set time. However, it is good practice to review how the student is progressing and whether the plan is working on an annual, or even quarterly, basis to ensure the plan can be changed if it is not successful.

2. If a parent refuses IDEA services, does a student automatically qualify for a 504 Plan?

    A. **No**. If a parent refuses special education services under the IDEA, the child is not automatically qualified for services under Section 504. However, the school district should consider evaluating the student and determining if program changes are required to prevent discrimination by the school based on the student's disability.

    > *Section 504 does not require a school to re-evaluate students on a 504 Plan annually, but annual or quarterly review of the efficacy of the plan is suggested in order to ensure a student's plan is being implemented & preventing discrimination.*

3. Is a school required to provide a 504 Plan for a student diagnosed with alcoholism?

    A. **Potentially**. A student with a diagnosis of alcoholism is considered disabled for the purposes of Section 504, but an evaluation will determine whether the student requires a 504 Plan in order to avoid discrimination.

4. Is a school required to provide a 504 Plan for a student who is a drug addict?

    > *Active illegal drug and alcohol use are treated differently under Section 504. A student actively using drugs is not covered by Section 504, while a student actively using alcohol is covered. On the other hand, past alcohol and drug use are both covered by Section 504.*

    A. **No**. A student actively using drugs is not covered by Section 504. However, a student who: (1) successfully completes drug rehabilitation and is no longer engaging in the illegal use of drugs; (2) is participating in a supervised rehabilitation program and is no longer engaging in such use; or (3) is erroneously regarded as engaging in such use but is not using illegal drugs, is considered to be a person with a disability. If a student meets one of the criteria listed above, the school must conduct an evaluation to determine whether a 504 Plan is required in order to avoid discrimination.

5. Do any physical or mental impairments lead to an automatic qualification for a 504 Plan?

    > *Although no physical or mental impairments automatically qualify a student for a 504 Plan, several conditions will almost always result in a student being covered by section 504.*

    A. **No**. Although several physical or mental impairments lead to the automatic finding that an individual has a disability (e.g. cancer), a school must complete an evaluation for each individual student to determine whether a 504 Plan is required in order to avoid discrimination.

DETERMINING IF A SECTION 504 PLAN IS REQUIRED

Defining Discrimination

What Actions are Discriminatory under Section 504?

Under Section 504, a school discriminates against a student when it:

1. Denies a student with a disability the opportunity to participate in or benefit from an aid, benefit, or service provided by the school district.

2. Fails to afford a student with a disability an opportunity to participate in or benefit from the aid, benefit, or service that is equal to the opportunity afforded non-disabled students.

3. Fails to provide a student with a disability an aid, benefit, or service that is as effective as that provided to non-disabled students.

4. Provides different or separate aids, benefits, or services to students with disabilities or to any class of disabled students, unless such action is necessary to provide the students with aid, benefits, or services that are as effective as those provided to non-disabled students.

5. Aids or perpetuates discrimination against a student with a disability by providing significant assistance to an agency, organization, or person that discriminates on the basis of a disability.

6. Denies a student with a disability the opportunity to participate as a member of planning or advisory boards.

7. Otherwise limits a student with a disability in the enjoyment of any right, privilege, advantage, or opportunity enjoyed by non-disabled students receiving an aid, benefit, or service.

8. Makes site or facility selections which effectively exclude persons with disabilities, denies them the benefits of an education, or otherwise subjects them to discrimination. 34 C.F.R. § 104.4(b).

What Does Equally Effective Mean?

Equally effective educational opportunities **does not** mean identical. The implementing regulations for Section 504 state that:

Aids, benefits, and services, to be equally effective, are not required to produce the identical result or level of achievement for disabled and non-disabled students, but must afford students with disabilities equal opportunity to obtain the same result, to gain the same benefit, or to reach the same level of achievement, in the most integrated setting appropriate to the student's needs. 34 C.F.R. § 104.4(b)(2).

Does a Disabled Student Have a Right to Participate in Programs for Non-Disabled Students?

Yes. Even if a school district provides separate or different programs or services for students with disabilities as allowed by Section 504, the school district must also allow a disabled student the opportunity to participate in those programs and services geared toward non-disabled students. 34 C.F.R. § 104.4(b)(3). On the other hand, Section 504 does not require programs to be fundamentally altered. 29 U.S.C. § 794. For example, a student with a disability can try out for the school's hockey team even though an adapted hockey program may be available. The student might require some program changes such as the rules being pre-taught that enable the student to participate but do not fundamentally alter the program. Academic examples would include admitting a student to an Advanced Placement ("AP") class even though a regular course might be available and may be one that the student could earn a higher grade in. The student with a disability must be allowed access to the AP courses like her peers. However, if the student is not able to skate up right but uses a sled with skate rails instead, the student would require fundamentally altering the hockey program before he could compete. Section 504 does not demand this from schools. Another example would be allowing a student who uses a racing wheelchair to compete against students in track. The use of the wheelchair would fundamentally change the competition and therefore, the student would not be permitted to participate.

FAPE Requirement under Section 504

Section 504 requires that students with disabilities be provided with a free appropriate public education (FAPE). The regulations require identification, evaluation, provisions of appropriate accommodations, and procedural safeguards. These requirements are similar to, though generally less stringent than, the requirements under the IDEA.

What is a Free Appropriate Public Education?

A free appropriate public education under Section 504 means regular or special education and related services and aids that are designed: (1) to meet individual educational needs of a student with a disability **as adequately as** the needs of nondisabled students are met; and (2) are designed in accordance with Section 504 procedures. 34 C.F.R. § 104.33(b)(1). Here, the focus is on accessing the general education rather the IDEA standard of providing special education services. Although Section 504 and the IDEA are different, implementing an Individualized Education Program (IEP) under the IDEA is one means of meeting the 504 standard. 34 C.F.R. § 104.33(b)(2). However, FAPE is generally achieved through implementation of a 504 Plan.

Educational Setting – Least Restrictive Environment

A school district must educate students with disabilities with students who are not disabled to the maximum extent appropriate to the needs of the disabled student. The student must be placed in the general education environment unless it is demonstrated that the student cannot be educated satisfactorily in the general environment with the use of supplementary aids and services. 34 C.F.R. § 104.34.

Accommodations, Modifications, and Program Changes

Generally, when a student is receiving special education and related services, the student is receiving them pursuant to an IEP. As a result, most non-IDEA qualified students with disabilities are on a 504 Plan that sets for the accommodations and modifications which will be provided to the student. These accommodations and modifications are necessary to allow the student to participate in class, learn the material, or to take the test. A discussion of 504 accommodations and modifications follows in the section below.

CAUTION: Under Section 504 students are entitled to any program change that they need to prevent discrimination. This includes special education, related services & other changes.

Accommodations under Section 504

The Section 504 regulations do not define the terms accommodation and modification as applied to school-age children. However, the Minnesota Department of Education ("Minnesota Department of Education") Manual on Section 504 defines accommodation as "adjustments and /or modifications that enable the learner to have equal access and opportunity to benefit from the educational program." MDE Manual on Section 504 (https://education.mn.gov/MDE/dse/504/).

Generally, **accommodations** are those changes that do not fundamentally alter or lower the standard being taught (i.e. do not affect course content/curriculum), while **modifications** are those changes which do fundamentally alter or lower the standard being taught (i.e. do affect course content/curriculum). *See* Miriam Freedman, J.D., School Law and Reform (June 2007); *see also* OCR Guidance on Report Cards and Transcripts, (October 2008) ("In general, accommodations do not affect course content or curriculum"). A state must ensure that "a child with a disability is not removed from education in age-appropriate regular classrooms solely because of needed modifications in the general education curriculum." 34 C.F.R. § 300.116(e).

<u>What are Possible Accommodations?</u>

Accommodations may involve changes in a number of different areas such as instructional strategies, behavioral management, environmental strategies, and organizational changes. The table below illustrates examples of accommodations.

• Provide lessons on tape or digital recording so the student can listen more than once	• Ask the student to repeat directions/assignments to ensure understanding	• Use tape recorders, computer-aided instruction, and other audio/visual equipment
• Provide outlines or study guides	• Modify test delivery (length of time, read questions, digital or tape record answers, segments)	• Alter time expectations for assignments

35

• Require fewer drill and practice activities	• Tailor homework assignments	• Provide cues, such as clock faces, indicating beginning and ending times
• Give both oral and visual instructions for assignments	• Change learner seating	• Use a study carrel
• Use peer tutors or cross-age tutors	• Use one-to-one tutorials	• Modify policy to allow increased number of excused absences for health reasons

MDE Manual on Section 504, MDE 2009.

<u>What are Possible Modifications?</u>

Course content and instructional goals and/or outcomes may need to be changed. The chart below outlines some examples of modifications.

• Select modified textbooks or workbooks	• Modify lesson or unit plan
• Tailor homework assignments	• Allow grade for attainment of alternate goals or outcomes

MDE Manual on Section 504, MDE 2009.

<u>What Medical Services Must be Provided?</u>

Section 504 provides that health services are included among those services that may be required to be provided to a student with a disability. 34 C.F.R. § 104.37(a)(2). The IDEA also states that school health services can be provided but does not require the provision of "medical services" other than for diagnostic and evaluation purposes. 20 U.S.C. § 1401(26). The Supreme Court has narrowly defined the scope of "medical services" that schools need not provide under the IDEA. Services that may be provided by a qualified school nurse or other qualified person are considered related services, which must be provided, rather than a medical service, which is not required. *Cedar Rapids Cmty. Sch. Dist. v. Garret F., ex rel. Charlene F.*, 526 U.S. 66 (1999).

Excluded medical services generally are those which must be provided by a licensed physician. Providing a supply of medication for a student is considered a medical service. *See* 34 C.F.R. Part 300,

Attachment 1, Analysis of Comments and Changes, 64 Fed. Reg. 12540 (1999) (considering IDEA). While Section 504 and the ADA do not provide for an explicit "medical services" exception like the IDEA, a court would likely treat the laws similarly in this area, i.e., medical services not required under IDEA would likely also not be required under 504 and the ADA.

> **Medical services that are necessary in school must generally be provided unless they are personal (such as the purchase of personal devices such as hearing aids, glasses). Medical services that can only be provided by a physician are not required.**

Grading, Transcripts, and Graduation

<u>Modified Grades</u>

Under Section 504, a student with disabilities may receive a modified curriculum and grade. Because Section 504 is a non-discrimination statute, this is true only insofar as modified grades are available to non-disabled students. Also, the grading scheme must be in response to the student's individual needs as opposed to an alternative system used for all, or only, disabled students.

For example, an IEP team or a 504 team may decide that the student will be graded on attainment of IEP goals, or the team may decide that the student will take a course pass/fail or not receive a grade. Modified grades and/or curriculum must be discussed with the parent and the team. Ensure that the parent has sufficient information about modifications to fully participate in the decision making process.

<u>Transcripts</u>

Generally, it is permissible to indicate **on a report card** that a student had taken a special education course, but it is not permissible to indicate this information **on a transcript**. This is because report cards are generally understood to be shared only with parents and within the school, while transcripts may be shared with outside entities such as colleges and employers. Identifying courses as being special education or otherwise on transcripts only for students with disabilities would disclose disability status. This constitutes differing treatment on the basis of disability in violation of Section 504 and the ADA. OCR Guidance on Report Cards and Transcripts, October 2008.

Notations that a modified curriculum was provided for a course may be used on a **transcript** as long as such notations are also used with non-disabled students. A transcript's purpose is to inform employers and universities about an applicant's academic credentials and achievements. If a transcript notation is consistent with this purpose and does not reveal a student's disability status, the notation is permissible. The U.S. Department of Education, Office of Civil Rights states:

Transcript notations concerning enrollment in different classes, course content, or curriculum by students with disabilities would be consistent with similar transcript designations for classes such as advanced placement, honors, and basic and remedial instruction, which are provided to both students with and without disabilities and thus would not violate Section 504 or Title II.

OCR Guidance on Report Cards and Transcripts, October 2008.

Notations on a **transcript** indicating a student had received **accommodations** are not permissible. This is because such notations generally do not reflect a student's academic credentials and achievement, but instead are generally understood to include aids and adjustments made only for disabled students. Accordingly, such notations appear to serve no other purpose than to identify a student as having a disability. This constitutes discrimination, i.e., differing treatment on the basis of disability. *See*, OCR Guidance on Report Cards and Transcripts, October 2008.

Graduation

A 504 Team or an IEP Team can override the school district or state requirements for graduation. A student's team may decide that the student needs: (1) accommodations in a general education course (no change in rigor); (2) that the student needs modifications in that course (change in rigor); or (3) that the student should not complete that requirement because of the disability. To ensure that the parent has informed consent, and that the team does not unintentionally discriminate, these decisions should be carefully reviewed at a team meeting and the results communicated to the parent in writing.

Q&A: Determining if a Section 504 Plan is Required

1. What is the difference between FAPE under Section 504 and FAPE under the IDEA?

    A. Under **Section 504**, FAPE requires schools to meet the needs of disabled individuals as adequately as the district meets the needs of nondisabled students, in accordance with Section 504 procedures. Under the **IDEA**, FAPE focuses on special education services. Section 504 requires the district to provide aids, services, and accommodation that allow the child to access regular education as adequately as typical peers.

    > *Least Restrictive Environment:*
    > *One goal of Section 504 is to provide program changes necessary to allow the student to be in the general education environment alongside non-disabled peers to the maximum extent possible.*

2. What is the difference between an accommodation and a modification?

    A. **Accommodations** are changes which do not affect course content/curriculum, while **modifications** are changes which do affect course content/curriculum.

3. If a student does not complete a required course (e.g. math), may the student receive a diploma?

    > *Modified Grades:*
    > *Modified grades and/or curriculum must be discussed with the parent/team. Ensure that the parent has sufficient information about modifications to fully participate in the decision making. process.*

    A. **Yes**. The student may receive a diploma if the team has determined that the student receives accommodations, modifications or waives the course that student would receive a regular diploma. Students with disabilities may not receive an alternative diploma or one that indicates they have a disability.

4. Can a student who is not graduating participate in graduation ceremonies?

    A. **Yes**. The student may participate if they meet the criteria to participate in the ceremony.

PROCEDURAL REQUIREMENTS

Procedural Requirements under Section 504

Section 504 imposes a variety of procedural requirements on school districts. These procedural requirements are generally not as onerous as those imposed under the IDEA. In particular, the 504 regulations give school districts significant discretion in regard to the amount and type of documentation created in conjunction with a student's 504 Plan.

Policy and Written Assurance of Nondiscrimination

A school district must have a school board policy of nondiscrimination under Section 504 and must provide written assurance of nondiscrimination to the U.S. Department of Education. 34 C.F.R. §104.5. Booth Law Group LLC has a sample policy.

Section 504 Administrator

Section 504 requires school districts to name a 504 Coordinator who is responsible for ensuring that the 504 policy is being implemented. 34 C.F.R. § 104.7(a).

Notice of Nondiscrimination

Notice that the district does not discriminate on the basis of disability must be provided to students, parents, employees, unions, and professional organizations. 34 C.F.R. § 104.8(a). The Notice **must** identify the school district's 504 Coordinator. The Notice **may** be published in newspapers, posted on the district's official bulletin board, included in annual school district publications (such as calendars), or disseminated by other written means.

Grievance Procedures

The school district must adopt grievance procedures to resolve complaints of discrimination. 34 C.F.R. § 104.7(b). Section 504 does not set forth the specific grievance procedures which must be utilized by schools, but rather allows each district to adopt its own set of grievance procedures. Students, parents, employees, and other individuals who believe their rights have been violated may file grievances.

Grievances may be filed with the school district or directly with the U.S. Department of Education, Office for Civil Rights. MDE has opined that the grievance procedures must include specific timelines.

Child Find

The school district **must** annually actively seek out and identify those learners not currently attending public school who may be eligible for accommodations under Section 504. 34 C.F.R. § 104.32. This obligation is termed "child find." Child find may be done through pre-school screening, outreach to parochial and other private schools, outreach to home-school parents, etc.

The "child find" requirement even applies within district schools themselves. Teachers, nurses, and counselors should be ready to make referrals for possible 504 evaluations based on personal observations of a student's behavior and performance or information received from parents or others. *See Hamilton Heights (IN) Sch. Corp.*, 37 IDELR 130 (OCR 2002) (finding Section 504 satisfied where referrals were made by teachers, nurses, and counselors, based on personal observations of the students' behaviors, requests from parents, and information from physicians).

In *Compton Unified Sch. Dist. v. Addison*, 598 F.3d 1181 (9th Cir. 2010), the Ninth Circuit Court of Appeals ruled that a school district violated IDEA's "child find" requirement when the school district failed to identify and evaluate a student already attending the public high school. Thus, even though the child find obligation is generally considered to apply to non-public school children, school districts should train staff to actively look for and report students that may need services or accommodations. This is true even where the parent is hesitant or disinclined to explore the possibility of services/accommodations, as in this case. Make sure parents have a written copy of the 504/IDEA procedural safeguards.

In *Fayette Cnty. (KY) Sch. Dist.*, 45 IDELR 67 (OCR 2005), the district violated Section 504 by failing to evaluate a student with diabetes who had recently transferred into the district. Even though the student received health care services under a school health care plan, he was experiencing depression and behavior problems and had attempted suicide, indicating the need for a 504 evaluation. We would recommend schools consider an IDEA evaluation in such a case.

<u>Annual Notice to Leaners with Disabilities</u>

The school district is required annually to take appropriate steps to notify all learners with disabilities, and parents or guardians, of the school district's duties under Section 504. 34 C.F.R. § 104.32(b).

<u>Notice Prior to Initial Evaluation and any Subsequent Change</u>

The school district is required to provide parental notice prior to conducting an initial evaluation for a student. Additionally, whenever a school district proposes to change the identification, evaluation, or educational placement of a student under 504, the parent must be provided with notice. The notice must include the following procedural safeguards:

1. Notice of the student/parent rights;

2. The opportunity to examine relevant records;

3. An impartial hearing with opportunity for participation by the parent and representation by counsel; and

4. A review procedure.

34 C.F.R. § 104.36.

<u>Records and Complaint Procedures</u>

Section 504 gives parents the right to examine the student's 504 file and any other relevant records. 34 C.F.R. § 104.36. Parents have the right to an impartial hearing with respect to the district's actions regarding their child's identification, evaluation, or educational placement. This includes the opportunity for parental participation in the hearing and representation by an attorney. 34 C.F.R. § 104.36. If the parent disagrees with the decision of the impartial hearing officer, the parent can seek review of that decision by a court of competent jurisdiction. 34 C.F.R. § 104.36.

On Section 504 matters other than FAPE, the parent has the right to file a complaint with the district's Section 504 Coordinator, who must investigate the allegations to the extent warranted by the nature of the complaint in an effort to reach a prompt and equitable resolution. 34 C.F.R. § 104.7. In a recent

U.S. Supreme Court case, it was determined that a parent does not need to exhaust the IDEA's administrative requirements where "the gravamen of the plaintiff's suit is something other than the denial of the IDEA's core guarantee of a FAPE." *Fry v. Napoleon Cmty. Schools*, 137 S.Ct. 743, 748 (2017). In other words, the IDEA's exhaustion requirements only apply to cases where a parent alleges a denial of a FAPE. The parent also has the right to file any complaint with the Office for Civil Rights ("OCR").

Step by Step Procedures to Create and Implement a 504 Plan

The process of identifying and planning for the needs of a student with a disability is an interactive process between school personnel and parents. Medical information about the student's condition and medical treatment regimen developed by the student's physician often serves as a basis for determining what health care services or accommodations will be provided. Once this information is presented, parents and school officials discuss how to accommodate the student's needs and implement the medical plan, if any. The student may also participate in the process if he or she has the desire and maturity. The remainder of this section will address, step by step, the procedures to implement a 504 Plan.

Identification and Referral

A parent, teacher, counselor, social worker, nurse, principal, or other person concerned that a student may have a disability that requires some program changes should refer the student to the appropriate school committee (e.g., child study team) for identification and evaluation of the student's individual education needs. The school committee should be composed of persons knowledgeable about the student, the student's school history, the student's individual needs, the meaning of evaluation data, and the placement options.

The school committee should consider the referral, including a review of the student's existing records (academic, social and behavioral), and consider evidence or documentation that the student may have a disability that warrants further evaluation under the 504 procedure. If the school or parent requests a 504 evaluation, the district's 504 coordinator (or school's 504 facilitator) should be notified so that notice of procedural rights, consent for evaluation, and necessary release of information forms can be sent to the parent.

Assessment/Evaluation

Evaluation of the student and formulation of an accommodation plan should be carried out by a 504 team composed of the student's teachers, and other persons knowledgeable of the student's needs. The 504 team will evaluate the nature of the student's suspected disability and the impact of the disability upon the student's education. The evaluation **should include** consideration of any behaviors that interfere with regular participation of the student in the educational program and/or activities. The evaluation **may include** consideration of family history, medical, psychological, social/emotional, and other relevant data concerning the student.

The 504 Team will invite the parent or guardian of the student to participate in a meeting or to provide input through other means concerning eligibility under Section 504 prior to making a final decision of eligibility. School personnel should ask the parent to provide medical or other information and authorizations required to establish the child's need for services and how to meet those needs. This information might include:

1. Information establishing the child's medical diagnosis, if any;

2. Description of the health care services required at school;

3. In the case of diabetes, physician and parent confirmation as to the student's ability to self-monitor blood glucose or self-administer insulin, if appropriate;

4. Parent medical authorization for administering medication and providing other medical care services at school;

5. Physician's order (sometimes called a Medical Management Plan); or

6. Consent to disclose information, both medical and educational, to the student's physician.

A final decision of eligibility should be made by the 504 team and communicated in writing to the parent, along with notification of the Section 504 procedural safeguards available to them, including the right to an impartial hearing and review.

504 Plan

When it has been determined that the student is eligible for and in need of educational accommodations, the 504 team will be responsible for determining what program changes are needed. In making such determination, the 504 team will consider all available relevant information, drawing upon a variety of sources. The parents or guardian will be invited to participate in the 504 team meetings where program changes for the student will be determined and will be given an opportunity to examine all relevant records.

The 504 team will develop a written plan describing the disability and the special accommodations needed. The plan will specify how the program changes will be provided, and by whom. The 504 team may determine that no program changes are required for the student. If so, the record of the 504 team's proceedings will reflect the identification of the student as having a disability and will state the basis for the decision that no special accommodations are presently needed.

The student should be served in the regular educational environment of the school, with the provision of the accommodations identified, unless the school demonstrates that such placement cannot be achieved satisfactorily. The 504 team will notify the parent in writing of its final 504 Plan and all school personnel who work with the student will be informed of the plan.

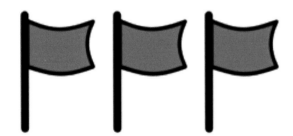

CAUTION: *Keep in mind that the duty to prevent discrimination is the school district's duty.* The district does not need the parent's permission to put a plan into place that will prevent the student from being discriminated against in school programming. The district should offer what it believes are appropriate program changes after receiving parental input. The school district should implement the 504 plan while discussing additional changes with parents. Parents may also file a grievance with the 504 coordinator if necessary.

Review of Student Progress

The 504 Team will monitor the progress of the student and the effectiveness of the student's education plan, and that the student's needs are being met as adequately as the needs of non-disabled students. Prior to any subsequent significant change in placement, a comprehensive reevaluation of the student's needs must be conducted.

Notice to Parents

The parents should be notified in writing of all decisions concerning the identification, evaluation, or educational placement of students made under these procedures. The parents should also be notified that they may examine relevant records. The parents should be informed that they have the right to an impartial hearing if they disagree with any decisions made by the 504 Team, with opportunity for participation by the parents and their counsel.

Documentation

Copies of all documents related to the identification, evaluation, or educational placement of the student should be maintained. Copies of all documents should be given to the parents upon request.

Implementing the Plan

All staff with a need to know information in the student's 504 plan (e.g., teachers, lunch room staff, coaches, and after-care program providers) should be provided a copy of the 504 plan. If questions arise as to the appropriateness of the medical treatment plan at school, the school nurse or other appropriate personnel should contact the student's physician. Neither Section 504 nor the Americans with Disabilities Act (ADA) are violated by confirming the correct treatment for a student.

A school may legitimately confirm the appropriateness of medication dosages and may refuse to administer a child's medication where the prescribed dosage is contrary to established protocols because of concerns about the student's health and the school's own liability. *See Davis v. Francis Howell Sch. Dist.*, 138 F.3d 754, 756 (1998) (holding the ADA was not violated where a school refused to administer Ritalin to child whose dosages exceed the Physician's Desk Reference recommendation).

Q&A: Procedural Requirements

1. Do school districts have to provide a 504 coordinator at each building?

   A. **No.** Although not required by the regulations, large school districts often identify a 504 Facilitator at each building or program to facilitate and monitor the identification, evaluation and provision of 504 accommodations to eligible students at the site.

2. Is there a difference between providing procedural safeguards under the IDEA and Section 504?

   A. **Yes.** If a student is qualified for services under both 504 and IDEA, the school district must satisfy the procedural safeguards of the IDEA. For students who are covered under 504 but not IDEA, the school district may choose to have a more simplified set of procedures. Both sets of procedures must be in writing, be provided to the parent, and followed by the school.

   > *The parents should be notified in writing of all decisions concerning the identification, evaluation, or educational placement of students made under these procedures.*

3. What is a district's child find obligation?

   A. The school district must annually actively seek out and identify those learners **not currently attending public school** who may be eligible for accommodations under Section 504. The child find requirement also applies **within a district's own schools**. Districts should train staff to refer individuals for a 504 evaluation, when, based on observation, it is possible the student may be eligible for a 504 Plan.

4. If a district wants to change a Student's 504 Plan, must the parents be notified?

   A. **Yes.** Whenever a school district proposes to change the identification, evaluation, or educational placement of a student under 504, the parents must be provided with notice.

5. What school staff and faculty should have access to a student's 504 Plan?

   A. All staff with a need to know information in the student's 504 Plan should be provided with a copy of the 504 Plan. Staff that need to know this information may include, but is not limited to, teachers, lunch room staff, coaches, and after care program providers.

ACCESS TO EXTRA-CURRICULAR AND NON-ACADEMIC PROGRAMS

Non-Discrimination in Athletics and Extra-Curriculars

The Section 504 regulations require school districts to provide non-academic and extra-curricular services and activities, including field trips and non-classroom activities, in a manner which affords disabled students an equal opportunity for participation in such services and activities. *See* 34 C.F.R. § 104.37.

Field Trips

<u>Do Not Impose Conditions for Attendance which Differ from Conditions Placed on Non-Disabled Students/Parents</u>

Schools must take steps to ensure that major changes to a student's program are provided during field trips. Additionally, schools are not allowed to charge parents additional fees for medical services or special accommodations which may be required to allow their child to attend the field trip with non-disabled peers. Similarly, schools may not condition the child's field trip opportunity on the parent's attendance.

Example: The parents of a sixth-grade student filed a complaint with the OCR after the school district placed certain conditions on their daughter's attendance at a multi-day field trip. The student had Type I diabetes and needed her blood sugar monitored. According to the parent's complaint, district staff told the parents that their daughter could attend the field trip only if one of the parents attended to provide the student's medical services and that they would have to pay their own registration fee. Later, the district decided to have another parent chaperone, who happened to be a nurse, to take care of the student's medical needs during the trip and asked the parents to sign a release form which authorized the other parent to provide the services.

The OCR found that the district had illegally discriminated against the student by placing conditions on her attendance. By conditioning the student's participation on the parents' willingness to pay additional expenses, take time to attend, or sign a written release allowing another parent to provide services, the school district treated the student differently than non-disabled peers, essentially limiting the student's equal participation in the field trip in violation of Section 504 and the ADA. *Clovis (CA) Unified Sch. Dist.*, 109 LRP 31672 (OCR 2009).

<u>Only Properly Documented, Significant Health or Safety Concerns Should Prevent Field Trip Attendance</u>

If the student's current medical condition presents an unacceptable risk to the student's health or safety, the school district may prohibit the student from going on the trip. However, this decision should not be made lightly and should involve the professional judgment of the school nurse, or the child's doctor.

Example: A student with cerebral palsy was prevented from attending an off-campus vocational training program on three days because on each of the days the student had experienced seizures which were not being effectively controlled with medication. The school nurse made the determination that attendance would be unsafe, recorded the relevant health information in the Nurse Log, and contacted the parents to inform them of her decision. On days when the student's seizure activity was effectively controlled by medication she was allowed to attend the off-campus activity. Given these circumstances, the OCR was unable to conclude that the school district had violated Section 504 or the ADA by excluding the student from the off-campus training experience. *North Hunterdon/Voorhees Reg'l (NJ) High Sch. Dist.*, 25 IDELR 165 (OCR 1996).

Compare: A ten-year-old third-grade student with mental impairment was excluded from participation in a field trip to a local television station. The primary reason advanced by the school district for her exclusion from the field trip was concern for the student's safety. The student had been diagnosed as having Niemann-Pick, a rare progressive neuro-degenerative disorder which affects motor, sensory, perceptual, and language functioning. Additionally, her doctor had advised that precautions be taken to protect her spleen and to avoid abdominal trauma.

Because of ambulatory problems resulting from the disorder and fear that the student might fall and injure herself, the student was escorted throughout the school building by an adult or student who would hold her hand so that she could maintain her balance. School officials also noted that the student's toileting skills and the academic appropriateness of the trip were factors in their decision to exclude her from the field trip. The OCR determined that the student was not afforded an equal opportunity to participate in the field trips in violation of 34 C.F.R. § 104.37(a)(1)-(2). The OCR noted that the student could have participated in the field trip if she had been provided the same accommodation that she is provided at school, i.e., an escort holding her hand. *Quaker Valley (PA) Sch. Dist.*, 352 IDELR 235 (OCR 1986).

Provide Equal Notice

School districts should ensure that parents of students with disabilities are provided the same notice about field trips as parents of nondisabled students. Failure to provide equal notice about field trips can result in illegal exclusion of students with disabilities. In *Mt. Gilead (OH) Exempted Village Sch. Dist.*, 20 IDELR 765 (OCR 1993), the OCR found the district's failure to provide written materials about a field trip to parents of students with disabilities denied the parents of the same opportunity afforded to parents of nondisabled students to make an informed decision about trip participation. *See also Quaker Valley (PA) Sch. Dist.*, 352 IDELR 235 (OCR 1986).

Extra-Curricular Activities

If a student needs accommodations to participate in an extra-curricular activity, those accommodations should be listed in the student's 504 Plan. The school district should have procedures in place to ensure that coaches, school club leaders, and other adults in charge of extra-curricular activities are made aware of needed accommodations. Activities sponsored by Parent-Teacher Organizations (PTOs) are generally not funded by the public school and the school district would not be required to provide accommodations for these activities. *Indep. Sch. Dist. No. 12, Centennial v. Minnesota Dep't. of Educ.*, 767 N.W.2d 478 (2009). For students on an IEP, extra-curricular activities (and accommodations necessary thereto) are to be considered by the IEP team. *Independent School Dist. No. 12, Centennial v. Minn. Dept. of Educ.*, 788 N.W.2d 907 (2010).

Physical Education and Athletics

Students with disabilities must be provided an equal opportunity to participate in physical education courses and interscholastic, club, or intramural athletics. A school district may offer separate or different physical education and athletic activities only if it is necessary for the student and only if no student with a disability is denied the opportunity to compete for teams or participate in courses that are not separate or different. 34 C.F.R. § 104.37(c)

Example: Swimming is included in the school district's regular physical education program for all third and sixth grade students. The swimming instruction is provided at the local YMCA. A total of 122 third and sixth-grade students participated in the swimming program during a particular school year. Of that total, 106 students were nondisabled and 16 were disabled.

The complainant's daughter, a third-grade student with mild mental impairment and a rare neuro-degenerative disorder, was the only student excluded from the swimming program. School officials excluded the student from the swimming program because the school principal felt that it was unsafe for her to participate. The school principal stated that the student was excluded because she was enrolled in an adaptive physical education program whereas swimming was provided in the regular physical education program.

The OCR determined that the school district violated Section 504 by failing to provide the student an equal opportunity to participate in the swimming program since there were accommodations which would have allowed her to participate. For instance, the school principal had stated that if the child had participated in the swimming class, she would have needed assistance in dressing and undressing and in getting from the locker room to the pool area because of her ambulatory difficulty. However, the school made no attempt to accommodate the student in swimming by providing the same accommodation with which she was provided while at school, i.e., someone to assist her. *Quaker Valley (PA) Sch. Dist.*, 352 IDELR 235 (OCR 1986).

Counseling Services

School districts should train counseling staff on the non-discrimination mandates imposed by Section 504. In particular, a school district must ensure that students with disabilities are not counseled toward more restrictive career objectives than are nondisabled students with similar interests and abilities. 34 C.F.R. § 104.37(b).

After School Care

School districts should ensure that parents of students with disabilities are not charged extra fees for after-school care when additional supervision or medical monitoring is required. Under Section 504, when a child with a disability applies to enroll in a non-educational program, a school district need not develop a special daycare program designed to meet the needs of children with disabilities. However, where a voluntary program is offered, on a free or tuition basis, children with disabilities may not be categorically excluded. They must be offered meaningful and equal access to that program. The same benefit must be offered meaningfully at the same cost to students with and without disabilities.

Children with disabilities may not be categorically excluded on the basis of their disabilities from non-educational programs, such as after-school programs. Such programs must reasonably accommodate children of disabilities, but can request documentation of the child's needs to identify proper accommodations. *Koester v. Young Men's Christian Ass'n of Greater St. Louis*, 855 F.3d 908, 912-13 (2017). Parents of such children may not be required to provide their own aides or babysitters to care for their children where the parents of children without disabilities are not subject to similar requirements. Finally, parents of such children may not be charged more than the parents of children without disabilities for their participation in the program. *Chattahoochee County (GA) Sch. Dist.*, 108 LRP 57787 (OCR 2008).

Q&A: Access to Extra-Curricular and Non-Academic Programs

1. May a school refuse to allow a student with a disability under Section 504 to go on a field trip?

Schools are not allowed to charge parents additional fees for medical services or special accommodations which may be needed to allow their child to attend the field trip with non-disabled peers.

A. **Not usually.** A school may refuse to allow a student with a disability to go on a field trip only if the student's current medical condition presents an unacceptable risk to the student's health or safety.

2. What notice must a school provide to a parent of a student with a disability about field trips?

A. **Equal notice** to that which the school provides to parents of students without disabilities. Failure to provide equal notice about field trips can result in illegal exclusion of students with disabilities.

3. Should accommodations for extra-curricular activities be listed in the 504 Plan?

A. **Yes**. Similarly, for students on an IEP, extra-curricular activities (and accommodations necessary thereto) are to be considered by the IEP team.

4. Must a school provide after school care for a child receiving services under Section 504?

School districts must ensure that students with disabilities are not counseled toward more restrictive career objectives than are nondisabled students with similar interests and abilities.

A. It depends. When a child with a disability applies to enroll in a non-educational program, a school district need not develop a special daycare program designed to meet the needs of children with disabilities. However, where a voluntary program is offered, on a free or tuition basis, children with disabilities may not be categorically excluded.

PTAs AND PTOs RESPONSIBILITIES

Parent Teacher Associations and Parent Teacher Organizations

Parent teacher associations ("PTAs") and parent teacher organizations ("PTOs") are generally not required to comply with the Americans with Disabilities Act and Section 504 of the Rehabilitations Act because they do not receive federal funds. However, if a school district provides "significant assistance" to a PTA or PTO sponsored activity, the school district could be held liable in the event that the PTA or PTO does not provide accommodations as required under the ADA and Section 504.[2] The Office for Civil Rights ("OCR"), the federal agency tasked with enforcing the ADA and Section 504, has looked at the following in considering whether a District has provided "significant assistance" to a PTO or a PTA:

1. Direct financial support

2. Indirect financial support

3. Provisions of tangible resources such as staff and materials

4. Intangible benefits such as the lending of recognition and approval

5. The selectivity of the recipient's provision of privileges and resources

6. Whether the relationship is occasional and temporary or permanent and long-term

Irvine (CA) Unified School District, 19 IDELR 883, 19 LRP 2145 (April 28, 1993). In the *Irvine case*, OCR determined that, although the Irvine Unified School District did not "fund or subsidize" the PTA Clubs programs, the District provided significant assistance because the PTA programs were located long-term in District buildings, the PTA programs used District classrooms and playing fields, the District did not charge the PTA for such use, and the District advertised PTA

---

[2] The Office for Civil Rights ("OCR") does not have jurisdiction pursuant to the ADA or Section 504 over an organization that does not receive federal financial assistance, such as a PTO or PTA. However, if the District provides significant assistance to a PTO or PTA, the OCR does have jurisdiction to investigate a District's violation(s) of the ADA and Section 504 in the event that the PTO or PTA does not make an activity or program accessible as defined by the ADA and Section 504.

programs on its website and school newsletter. *Id*. Therefore, OCR concluded that the District was liable

because the PTA's failed to provide accommodations as required by the ADA and Section

504, and the District continued to provide significant assistance to the PTA despite this failure. Id.

If a school district provides significant assistance to a private program or activity, the District

may be liable if that private program or activity fails to accommodates an individual as required by

the ADA and Section 504.

GRADING: TRANSCRIPTS AND REPORT CARDS

Report Cards

Report cards may identify special education or other resources that are provided to a student, as long as non-disability related services (for example, English language support, remedial courses, or gifted and talented services) are noted on the report card. Additionally, report cards may identify the level of the course as long as similar identifiers are used for non-special education students. For example, the report card may indicate that the course was "modified" or that the student received "accommodations" in the course. Courses **may not** be labeled "special education," but courses **can be** titled "basic," "honors," "advanced," "general," or some similar title.

A school must use the same report card form for students with disabilities and general education students. However, as a **small** exception to this rule, a school may not need to use the general report card if a student's unique needs make using the general report card ineffective in reporting the student's progress. *See Saddleack Valley (CA) Unified School District* 17 LRP 1353 (OCR 1990). Report cards and other forms of grading (for example, mid-term reports) must be provided as frequently for students with special needs as provided for general education students. A report card **does not** replace the need to provide the type and number of progress reports agreed to by the IEP team and delineated on the IEP.

Transcripts

Unlike report cards, transcripts **may not** contain information about special education services. They **may not** reflect that a student took a special education course. Transcripts may not show accommodations or modifications. Transcripts **may** identify the course as "basic," "level 1," and "practical." A transcript **may** reflect that a course was modified as long as that designation is used for remedial courses, gifted services, and other regular education courses. A school should avoid using terms such as "special education," "homebound instruction," "resource room," "requirement waived – medical," or "learning center" on a transcript.

According to the OCR, report cards and transcripts are treated differently because report cards are used to inform parents and guardians of student progress, while transcripts may be provided to others such as postsecondary institutions or potential employers. As a result, a school must not suggest to a third party that a person is disabled.

Grades, GPAs and Honor Rolls

Grades

An IEP team can determine that an alternative grading system will be used for a student with a disability. However, all special education students should not be automatically graded on an alternative basis, and the determination to use an alternative grading basis must be individually determined. A student with a disability in a general education course should be graded like his or her non-disabled peers.

Grades should not be impacted by a student having an accommodation that allows them to perform in the general education curriculum. For example, grades should not be impacted by the use of Braille materials, more time to complete work, or a test being read to a student. On the other hand, if the content or rigor of a course is changed, then a student's grade can be modified as a result.

GPAs and Honor Rolls

A school may use a weighted grading system to compute grade point averages ("GPAs"), honor roll, class rank, honor society, and other awards as long as the weighting is based on objective criteria. A school must not automatically weigh all special education courses differently than general education courses. The level of difficulty and student achievement may be taken into account when the school determines a student's GPA or an honor. *See Letter to Runkel*, 25 IDELR 387 (OCR 1996).

UNITED STATES DEPARTMENT OF EDUCATION

OFFICE FOR CIVIL RIGHTS

THE ASSISTANT SECRETARY

> The Office for Civil Rights in the United States Department of Education issues this guidance to provide state and local education agencies with information concerning disclosure of disability on report cards and transcripts for students with disabilities attending public elementary and secondary schools, under Section 504 of the *Rehabilitation Act of 1973* (29 U.S.C. § 794) and its implementing regulation (34 C.F.R. Part 104) and Title II of the *Americans with Disabilities Act of 1990* (42 U.S.C. § 12131 *et seq.*) and its implementing regulation (28 C.F.R. Part 35). As appropriate, this document also discusses two other relevant federal laws, the *Individuals with Disabilities Education Act of 2004* (20 U.S.C. § 1400 et seq.) and its implementing regulation (34 C.F.R. Part 300) and the *Family Educational Rights and Privacy Act* (20 U.S.C. §1232g) and its implementing regulation (34 C.F.R. Part 99).
>
> This guidance represents the Department's current thinking on this topic. It does not create or confer any rights for or on any person. This guidance does not impose any requirements beyond those required under applicable law and regulations.
>
> If you are interested in commenting on this guidance, please email us your comment at OCR@ed.gov or write to us at the following address: U.S. Department of Education; Office for Civil Rights; 400 Maryland Avenue, SW; Washington, DC 20202.

OCT 17 2008

Dear Colleague:

I am writing to you to address some issues concerning report cards and transcripts for students with disabilities attending public elementary and secondary schools. Through this letter and the enclosed Questions and Answers document, I am clarifying how federal laws apply to statements on report cards and transcripts when these statements identify students as students with disabilities.

The Office for Civil Rights (OCR) in the United States Department of Education (Department) has enforcement responsibilities under two of the applicable federal laws -- Section 504 of the *Rehabilitation Act of 1973* (Section 504) and Title II of the *Americans With Disabilities Act of 1990* (Title II). Section 504 prohibits discrimination on the basis of disability in programs or activities receiving Federal financial assistance, and Title II prohibits discrimination on the basis of disability by public entities, including public elementary and secondary school systems, regardless of receipt of Federal financial assistance. As part of their disability nondiscrimination mandates, Section 504 and Title II require local education agencies (LEAs) to provide a free appropriate public education (FAPE) to qualified individuals with disabilities in their jurisdiction. See 34 C.F.R. § 104.33 and 28 C.F.R. § 35.103(a).

Other federal laws are also relevant. Through the Office of Special Education and Rehabilitative Services (OSERS), the Department of Education administers the *Individuals with Disabilities Education Act (IDEA)*, which provides funds to states to assist in making FAPE available to

Our mission is to ensure equal access to education and to promote educational excellence throughout the nation.

eligible children with disabilities. *IDEA* requirements apply to state education agencies (SEAs), school districts, and other public agencies that serve *IDEA*-eligible children. The Department's Family Policy Compliance Office implements and enforces the *Family Educational Rights and Privacy Act* (*FERPA*). *FERPA* protects the privacy interests of parents and students with regard to education records, and generally prohibits a policy or practice of disclosing personally identifiable information from education records without consent unless it is subject to a specific exemption.

Report cards and transcripts convey information about students. LEAs issue report cards to parents to indicate their child's progress or level of achievement in specific classes, course content, or curriculum. These report cards are made available to parents, not to postsecondary institutions, potential employers, and others outside the LEA. In contrast, a student's transcript generally is intended to inform postsecondary institutions or prospective employers of a student's academic credentials and achievements. Accordingly, there is an expectation that a student's transcript could be shared with persons other than the student and the student's parents.

For students with disabilities, questions arise about whether the information conveyed by report cards and transcripts can include information about the students' disabilities, including whether those students received special education and related services. As discussed in the enclosed Questions and Answers document, under federal disability discrimination laws, the general principle is that report cards may contain information about a student's disability, including whether that student received special education or related services, as long as the report card informs parents about their child's progress or level of achievement in specific classes, course content, or curriculum, consistent with the underlying purpose of a report card.

However, transcripts may not contain information disclosing students' disabilities. Transcripts are provided to persons other than the student and the student's parents to convey information about a student's academic credentials and achievements. Information about a student's disability, including whether that student received special education or related services due to having a disability, is not information about a student's academic credentials and achievements. Therefore, transcripts may not provide information on a student's disability.

The enclosed Questions and Answers document provides additional information concerning the determination of what statements and notations may be used on report cards and transcripts for students with disabilities.

Compliance with Section 504 and Title II principles in reporting student achievement is one means of providing students with disabilities with equal educational opportunity. I look forward to continuing our work together to improve educational outcomes for all students with disabilities.

Sincerely,

Stephanie J. Monroe
Assistant Secretary for Civil Rights

Enclosure

United States Department of Education
Office for Civil Rights

October 2008

Questions and Answers on Report Cards and Transcripts For Students with Disabilities Attending Public Elementary and Secondary Schools

RELEVANT FEDERAL LAWS

1. **What federal laws can help address questions about what information about disability may appear on report cards and transcripts for students with disabilities attending public elementary and secondary schools?**

Section 504 and Title II - Section 504 of the *Rehabilitation Act of 1973* (Section 504) prohibits discrimination on the basis of disability in programs or activities receiving Federal financial assistance. Title II of the *Americans With Disabilities Act of 1990* (Title II) prohibits discrimination on the basis of disability by public entities, including public elementary and secondary school systems, regardless of receipt of Federal financial assistance. The Office for Civil Rights (OCR) in the United States Department of Education (Department) has enforcement responsibilities under both of these laws.   As part of their disability nondiscrimination mandates, Section 504 and Title II require local education agencies (LEAs) to provide a free appropriate public education (FAPE) to qualified individuals with disabilities in their jurisdiction. See 34 C.F.R. § 104.33 and 28 C.F.R. § 35.103(a).

Section 504 and Title II do not have specific provisions addressing report cards or transcripts. The regulations implementing Section 504 and Title II make clear that in general, Section 504 and Title II prohibit recipients and public entities from treating persons differently on the basis of disability in the provision of aid, benefits, or services. However, recipients and public entities may provide a different aid, benefit, or service to persons with disabilities where necessary to provide an aid, benefit, or service that is as effective as that provided to others. See 34 C.F.R. § 104.4(b)(1)(i)-(iv) and 28 C.F.R. § 35.130(b)(1)(i)-(iv). Among the aid, benefits, and services provided to students and parents are report cards and transcripts. Section 504 and Title II do not contain specific confidentiality requirements, but do prohibit different treatment on the basis of disability. This generally would prohibit unnecessary disclosures of disability status to third parties.

Other federal laws are also relevant.

IDEA – Through the Office of Special Education and Rehabilitative Services (OSERS), the Department of Education administers the *Individuals with Disabilities Education Act* (*IDEA*), which provides funds to states to assist in making a free appropriate public education (FAPE) available to eligible children with disabilities. *IDEA* requirements apply to state education agencies (SEAs), school districts, and other public agencies that serve *IDEA*-eligible children.

IDEA does not have specific provisions on student report cards or transcripts, but does require that the individualized education program (IEP) for a child with a disability include a description of how the child's progress toward meeting the annual goals set forth in his or her IEP will be measured and when periodic reports on the child's progress toward meeting the annual goals will be provided (such as through the use of quarterly or other periodic reports, concurrent with the issuance of report cards). 20 U.S.C. § 1414(d)(1)(A)(i)(III); 34 C.F.R. § 300.320(a)(3). These periodic progress reports may be separate from, or included as part of, the regular report cards of students with disabilities with an IEP. In general, the nondiscrimination principles of Section 504 and Title II would apply to report cards with or without such progress reports.

FERPA - The Department's Family Policy Compliance Office implements and enforces the *Family Educational Rights and Privacy Act* (*FERPA*). *FERPA* protects the privacy interests of parents and students with regard to education records, and generally prohibits a policy or practice of disclosing personally identifiable information from education records without consent unless it is subject to a specific exception.

Disclosures of personally identifiable student information, including disability status, are subject to the protections of *FERPA* and *IDEA*. Generally, these statutes require consent prior to disclosures of personally identifiable information contained in education records unless a specific exception applies. See 34 C.F.R. §§ 99.30 - 99.31 of the *FERPA* regulations and 34 C.F.R. § 300.622 of the *IDEA* regulations. Both student report cards and student transcripts are considered "education records" under *FERPA* and *IDEA*.

While the primary focus of the following questions and answers are the requirements under Section 504 and Title II of the ADA, to the extent that IDEA applies, this law is briefly discussed as well.

REPORT CARDS

2. **May a report card for a student with a disability identify special education or other related services or resources being provided for that student or otherwise indicate that the student has a disability? For instance, may the report card refer to an IEP or a plan providing for services under Section 504?**

Yes. Report cards are provided to parents to indicate their child's progress or level of achievement in specific classes, course content, or curriculum. Consistent with this purpose, it would be permissible under Section 504 and Title II for a report card to indicate that a student is receiving special education or related services, as long as the report card informs parents about their child's progress or level of achievement in specific classes, course content, or curriculum. For instance, a report card for a student with a disability may refer to an IEP or a plan for providing services under Section 504 in order to report on the student's progress on the specific goals in the IEP or plan developed under Section 504.

However, the mere designation that a student has an IEP or is receiving a related service, without any meaningful explanation of the student's progress, such as a grade or other evaluative standard established by an LEA and/or SEA, would be inconsistent with *IDEA's* periodic reporting requirements, as well as with Section 504 and Title II. Under Section 504 and Title II, in general, the LEA must provide students with disabilities report cards that are as informative and effective as the report cards provided for students without disabilities. See 34 C.F.R. § 104.4(b)(1)(i)-(iv) and 28 C.F.R. § 35.130(b)(1)(i)-(iv). Without more meaningful information, a report card that indicates only special education status provides the student with a disability with a benefit or service that is different from and not as informative and effective as the benefit or service that is provided through the report card for students without disabilities.

3. **May a report card for a student with a disability distinguish between special education programs and services and general education curriculum classes through specific notations or the use of asterisks or other symbols?**

In general, yes. LEAs frequently distinguish between general education curriculum classes and other types of programs and classes, such as advanced placement, honors, or remedial classes. Making similar distinctions on report cards would be consistent with the general requirements of Section 504 and Title II that individuals with disabilities may not unnecessarily be treated differently than individuals without disabilities.

See 34 C.F.R. § 104.4(b)(1)(i)-(iv) and 28 C.F.R. § 35.130(b)(1)(i)-(iv). Under Section 504 and Title II, in order to properly reflect the progress of a student with a disability in a modified or alternate education curriculum, an LEA may distinguish between special education programs and services provided under a modified or alternate education curriculum and regular education classes under the general education curriculum on the student's report card. For instance, where a student's IEP calls for a modified tenth grade literature curriculum to be provided through the special education program, it would be appropriate for the report card to indicate that the student's progress was measured based on the modified education curriculum. This distinction also may be achieved by using an asterisk or other symbol meant to reference the modified or alternate education curriculum as long as the statements on the report card, including the asterisks, symbols or other coding, provide an explanation of the student's progress that is as informative and effective as the explanation provided for students without disabilities.

4.   **May special notations, including asterisks or other symbols, appear on a report card for a student with a disability who received accommodations in general education curriculum classes?**

Yes. Accommodations are generally understood to include aids or adjustments that are part of an IEP or plan developed under Section 504 and that enable the student with a disability to learn and demonstrate what the student knows. In general, accommodations do not affect course content or curriculum. Examples may include sign language interpreters in the classroom, the provision of materials in alternate formats, or extra time on tests. Accordingly, to the extent that the use of notations, asterisks, symbols, or other coding on a report card to indicate that a student with a disability received accommodations is part of the information given to parents about their child's progress or level of achievement in specific classes, course content, curriculum, the IEP, or the plan under Section 504, it is permissible under Section 504 and Title II.

5.   **May a report card for a student with a disability simply refer to another document that more fully describes the student's progress?**

Yes. Nothing in Section 504 or Title II requires that LEAs use any particular format or method to provide information to parents about their child's progress or level of achievement in specific classes, course content, curriculum, IEP, or plan under Section 504. As explained above, under Section 504 and Title II, the LEA must provide students with disabilities report cards that are as informative and effective as the report cards provided to students without disabilities. As noted above, there are also IDEA-specific provisions that require periodic reporting.

Office for Civil Rights
United States Department of Education

6. May report card grades for a student with a disability be based on grade level standards?

Yes. Assigning grades (i.e., achievement or "letter" grades) for a child with a disability based on the student's grade level (i.e., year-in-school) standards would not be inconsistent with Section 504 or Title II. Generally, Section 504 and Title II would require that students with and without disabilities in the same regular education classes in the general education curriculum be graded using the same standards. That is, if an LEA assigns grades to nondisabled students participating in regular education classes using grade level standards to reflect progress in the general education curriculum, then the LEA would also use those standards to assign grades to students with disabilities in those same classes. See 34 C.F.R. § 104.4(b)(1)(i)-(iv) and 28 C.F.R. § 35.130(b)(1)(i)-(iv). Nothing in Section 504 or Title II prohibits SEAs and LEAs from deciding how to establish standards to reflect the progress or level of achievement of students with disabilities who are taught using different course content or a modified or alternate education curriculum. To the extent that a student with a disability is not participating in regular education classes, but is receiving modified course content or is being taught under a modified or alternate curriculum, it would be up to the SEA and/or the LEA to determine the standards to be used to measure the student's progress or level of achievement.

TRANSCRIPTS

7. May a transcript for a student with a disability indicate that the student has a disability, has been enrolled in a special education program, or has received special education or related services?

No. A student's transcript generally is intended to inform postsecondary institutions or prospective employers of a student's academic credentials and achievements. Information that a student has a disability, or has received special education or related services due to having a disability, does not constitute information about the student's academic credentials and achievements. Under Section 504 and Title II, recipients and public entities may not provide different or separate aid, benefits, or services to individuals with disabilities, or to any class of individuals with disabilities, unless such action is necessary to provide those individuals with aid, benefits, or services that are as effective as those provided to others. See 34 C.F.R. § 104.4(b)(1)(i)-(iv) and 28 C.F.R. § 35.130(b)(1)(i)-(iv). Notations that are used exclusively to identify a student as having a disability or identify education programs for students with disabilities unnecessarily provide these students with different educational benefits or services. Identifying programs as being only for students with disabilities also would be viewed as disclosure of disability status of enrollees and constitutes different treatment on the basis of disability. Therefore, it would be a violation of Section 504 and Title II for a student's transcript to indicate that a student has received special education or a related service or that the student has a disability.

In addition, prohibiting such preadmission and preemployment disclosures is consistent with the Section 504 regulatory requirements that, in general, postsecondary institutions may not make preadmission inquiries as to whether an applicant for admission has a disability prior to admission, 34 C.F.R. § 104.42(b)(4), nor may employers conduct preemployment medical examinations or make preemployment inquiries as to whether an applicant for employment has a disability prior to an offer of employment, 34 C.F.R. § 104.14.

8. May a transcript for a student with a disability indicate, either through specific notations or the use of asterisks or other symbols, that the student took classes with a modified or alternate education curriculum?

In general, yes. While a transcript may not disclose that a student has a disability or has received special education or related services due to having a disability, a transcript may indicate that a student took classes with a modified or alternate education curriculum. This is consistent with the transcript's purpose of informing postsecondary institutions and prospective employers of a student's academic credentials and achievements. Transcript notations concerning enrollment in different classes, course content, or curriculum by students with disabilities would be consistent with similar transcript designations for classes such as advanced placement, honors, and basic and remedial instruction, which are provided for both students with and without disabilities, and thus would not violate Section 504 or Title II. This distinction may also be achieved by using an asterisk or other symbol meant to reference the modified or alternate education curriculum. These notations, asterisks, or other symbols indicating a modified or alternate education curriculum are permissible when they do not specifically disclose that a student has a disability, are not used for the purpose of identifying programs for students with disabilities, and are consistent with the purpose of a student transcript.

9. May special notations, including asterisks or other symbols, appear on a transcript for a student with a disability who received accommodations in general education curriculum classes?

In general, no. Because the use of accommodations generally does not reflect a student's academic credentials and achievement, but does identify the student as having a disability, it would be a violation of Section 504 and Title II for a student's transcript to indicate that the student received accommodations in any classes. For example, a notation indicating the use of Braille materials is not related to whether that student mastered all the tenth grade objectives for her literature class. The only purpose of such a notation is to identify that student as having a visual impairment. Because accommodations are generally understood to include aids and adjustments to enable a student with a disability to learn and demonstrate knowledge, this notation could identify the student as having a disability and therefore constitute different treatment on the basis of disability.

10. **May a transcript for a student with a disability indicate that a student received a certificate of attendance or similar document rather than a regular diploma?**

A transcript for a student with a disability may indicate receipt of a certificate of attendance or a similar document, rather than a regular diploma, under certain circumstances. These circumstances are where this does not disclose that a student has received special education or related services, does not otherwise specifically disclose that a student has a disability (for example, because certificates of attendance are available to both students with disabilities and students without disabilities), is not used for the purpose of identifying programs for students with disabilities, and is consistent with the purpose of a student transcript -- to inform postsecondary institutions and prospective employers of a student's academic credentials and achievements.

DEPARTMENT OF EDUCATION

Q&A: High School Graduation, Diplomas and Aging Out of Special Education Services for Students with Disabilities

The Minnesota Department of Education Division of Compliance and Assistance has developed this document to address questions raised by parents and school districts regarding high school diplomas for students with disabilities. The purpose of this document is to provide helpful, general information to the public. It does not constitute legal advice nor is it a substitute for consulting with a licensed attorney. The information below should not be relied upon as a comprehensive or definitive response to your specific legal question.

Question 1: Under what conditions may a student with a disability be exited from special education services?

Answer: A student with a disability may only be exited from special education under the following three conditions:

- If, after the completion of a special education evaluation, it is determined that the student is no longer a student with a disability;
- Upon a student's graduation from high school with a regular high school diploma; or
- Upon the student exceeding the maximum age for receiving special education services.

Authority: 34 C.F.R. § 300.306(a)(1); 34 C.F.R. § 300.102(a)(3)(i); 34 C.F.R. § 300.101(a); and Minn. Stat. § 125A.03

Question 2: Must a school district conduct an evaluation of a student with a disability when that student is ready to graduate from secondary school with a high school diploma?

Answer: No. A school district is not required to conduct an evaluation of a student with a disability when that student is ready to graduate from secondary school with a high school diploma. Rather, graduation with a high school diploma automatically makes the student ineligible for services under Part B of the Individuals with Disabilities Education Act (IDEA) and Minnesota law.

Authority: 34 C.F.R. § 300.305(e)(2); Minn. Stat. § 125A.03(b)

Question 3: How does a school district inform parents that their student with a disability is eligible to graduate from high school?

Answer: If a school district believes that a student with a disability is on track to graduate, based upon meeting state and local graduation requirements, including passing graduation assessments, the school district must send the student's parent prior written notice proposing exiting the student through graduation with a high school diploma.

Authority: 34 C.F.R. § 300.503(a)(1)

Question 4: Does a parent of a student with a disability have the ability to object to the district's proposed graduation of the student with a high school diploma?

Answer: The parent of a student with a disability may object to the proposed change of placement if the parent does not believe the student has or will meet the necessary state and local requirements for high school graduation by the end of the school year, and/or if the parent does not believe that the student has met his or her IEP goals and objectives, which include transition goals.

For students who struggled academically, the courts and hearing officers have determined that the school district must meet a two-part test in order to exit a student based upon high school graduation. First, the student must have met the state and local requirements for high school graduation. Second, the student's IEP must be reasonably calculated to provide the student with some educational benefit in each of the transition areas, if appropriate.

Authority: Minn. Stat. § 120B.024(a); Minn. Stat. § 120B.30, Subd. 1(c). *See* 2002 WL 433061 (N.D. Ill.) (Cited Chuhran v. Walled Lake Consol. Sch. 830 F. Supp. 465, 474 (E.D. Mich. 1993), affd. 51 F. 3rd 271 (6th Cir. 1995)). *See* also Quabbin Regional Sch. Dist., 44 IDELR 56 (SEA Mass. 2005); 54 IDELR 283, (U.S. Dist. Ct. Mass. 2010); Black River Falls Sch. Dist., 40 IDELR 163 (SEA WI 2004)

Question 5: What must a district provide to a student with a disability whose eligibility under Part B of the IDEA terminates upon graduation?

Answer: When a student with a disability graduates from secondary school, the school district must provide that student with a summary of his or her academic achievement and functional performance. This summary must include recommendations on how to assist the student in meeting his or her postsecondary goals.

Authority: 34 C.F.R. § 300.305(e)(2),(3); 34 C.F.R. § 300.102(a)(3)(iv); Minn. Stat. § 125A.03(b)

Question 6: Does a student's eligibility for special education end with receipt of an alternative degree such as a certificate or a general educational development credential (GED)?

Answer: No. As used in 34 C.F.R. § 300.305(e)(2), the term "regular high school diploma" does not include an alternative degree that is not fully aligned with the state's academic standards, such as a certificate or a general educational development credential (GED).

Authority: 34 C.F.R. § 300.102(a)(3)(iv)

Question 7: What is an "IEP-driven diploma?"

Answer: An "IEP-driven diploma" is the colloquial reference used to describe the diploma earned by a student with a disability when the objectives in that student's individualized education program (IEP) are the factors used to determine whether he or she receives a diploma.

The requirement that school districts grant a high school diploma to a student with a disability when these objectives are met is codified in Minnesota law. "Upon completion of secondary school or the equivalent, a pupil with a disability who satisfactorily attains the objectives in the pupil's IEP must be granted a high school diploma that is identical to the diploma granted to a pupil without a disability."

Authority: Minn. Stat. § 125A.04; *See* Letter to Anonymous, 22 IDELR 456 (OSEP 1994)

Question 8: When is it appropriate for a student with a disability to receive a diploma based on attainment of IEP objectives, and who should make this decision?

Answer: The student's IEP team, including the parent(s), is charged, in part, with determining appropriate placement, accommodations, modifications, services, goals, objectives, transition goals, objectives, and services for that student. In making these determinations, the IEP team also considers whether the student is able to take the examinations required or fulfill all of the requirements necessary for graduation in Minnesota, with or without modification. For some students, the IEP team may decide that attainment of individualized objectives is a more appropriate determining factor, with respect to receipt of a high school diploma, than is attainment of required examinations or other requirements. The IEP team, because of its unique knowledge of and work with the student, is best suited to make this determination. The student's parent must consent to the proposed change of placement prior to exiting the student.

Authority: 34 C.F.R. §§ 300.320; 300.321; 300.324; 300.503; Minn. Stat. § 125A.091, Subd. 3a; Minn. Stat, § 125A.08(a)(1); Minn. R. 3525.2810, subp. 2-4

Question 9: Does a diploma or transcript earned by a student with a disability differ in appearance than that earned by a student without a disability?

Answer: Minnesota law requires that such a diploma be identical to the diploma granted to a student without a disability. The transcript and diploma of a student with a disability may not contain information disclosing that the student has a disability. A notation that the student's diploma was IEP-driven is considered such a disclosure. Such action is considered different treatment based on disability and is prohibited under federal law.

The transcript of a student with a disability can indicate that the student took classes with a modified or alternate curriculum when the indication, through notation or symbols, does not disclose that the student has a disability and is not used to identify programs for students with disabilities. Such transcript notations must also be consistent with the transcript's purpose of providing information on the student's academic achievements. Note that transcripts must not include notations indicating that a student received accommodations in the general education curriculum.

Authority: 34 C.F.R. § 104.4(b)(1)(i)-(iv); 28 C.F.R. § 35.130(b)(1)(i)-(iv); 28 C.F.R. § 35.130(b)(1)(i)-(iv); Minn. Stat. § 125A.04; Minn. R. 3525.2810, subp. 2-4; Dear Colleague Letter: Report Cards and Transcripts for Students with Disabilities, U.S. Department of Education, Office for Civil Rights (October 17, 2008)

Question 10: If a student is enrolled in a nonresident district, either through placement by their resident district to assure appropriate services or through an enrollment option program, which district awards the diploma once graduation criteria has been met and the IEP team recommends graduation?

Answer: If the student is open enrolled, the enrolling district awards the diploma. If the student is attending an area learning center program in the nonresident district, the student can choose to receive the diploma from either the resident district or the district where the area learning center is located. Statutes do not address the award of a diploma where a student is placed by their resident district, but in those cases, while it would be logical for the resident district to award the diploma, alternately the enrolling district could award the diploma. For MARSS reporting purposes, the student is enrolled in the enrolling district; and the enrolling district will report to MDE that the student has graduated. The enrolling district will also code the student as a graduate.

Authority: Minn. Stat. § 124D.03, Subd. 9; Minn. Stat. § 123A.06, Subd. 4

Question 11: In Minnesota, at what age is a student with a disability no longer eligible for services?

Answer: The IDEA requires that a Free Appropriate Public Education (FAPE) be made available to all students with disabilities between the ages of 3 and 21, inclusive. With respect to the application of that requirement to students aged 3, 4, 5, 18, 19, 20, or 21, the IDEA defers to state law. In Minnesota, FAPE is available to all persons under the age of 21. The closely related right to FAPE for students with disabilities is expanded under state law to include students from birth until July 1 after the student with a disability turns 21. The expansion does not extend beyond secondary school or its equivalent except as under the state's graduation incentives program.

Authority: 34 C.F.R. § 300.101(a); 34 C.F.R. § 300.102(a)(1); Minn. Stat. § 120A.20, Subd. 1; Minn. Stat. § 125A.03(b); Minn. Stat. § 124D.68

Question 12: Is a student with a disability, who is still enrolled in high school, eligible for services in the upcoming school year if the student turns 21 during the summer?

Answer: Special instruction and services must be provided from birth until July 1 after the student with a disability becomes 21 years old.

Authority: 34 C.F.R. §§ 300.101(a); 300.102(a)(1); Minn. Stat. § 120A.20, Subd. 1; Minn. Stat. § 125A.03(b)

Q&A: Grading: Transcripts and Report Cards

1. Can a report card identify that a student received special education services?

   A. **Yes.** However, if the school identifies that a student receives special education services on a report card, the school must also note non-disability related services on a report card (for example, English language support or gifted and talented courses).

   > *Report cards and transcripts are treated differently because report cards are not generally provided to third parties, while transcripts are often given out to third parties.*

2. Can a transcript identify that a student received special education service?

   A. **No.** A transcript must not identify that a student received special education services, such as accommodations or modifications.

3. Can a school label a course as special education?

   A. **No. Neither report cards nor transcripts** may label courses as special education. Report cards may identify the level of the course, as long as similar identifiers are used for non-special education courses. Transcripts may identify the course as "basic," "level 1," and "practical."

   > *A school may use a weighted grade system to calculate GPAs and honor roll, but the weighting must be based on objective criteria, and the school may not automatically weight special education courses differently.*

4. May special education students be graded on an alternative basis?

   A. **It depends**. A student receiving special education services may be graded on an alternative grading system if the IEP team decides that an alternative system would be better for the student, but the decision should be made individually for each student.

5. May a transcript reflect that a course was modified?

   A. **Yes.** A transcript may state that a course was modified as long as the designation is used for remedial courses, gifted courses, or other regular education courses.

BULLYING AND HARASSMENT

Aug. 20, 2013

Dear Colleague:

The U.S. Department of Education's Office of Special Education and Rehabilitative Services (OSERS) is committed to working with States to ensure that school districts provide all children with positive, safe, and nurturing school environments in which they can learn, develop, and participate. OSERS is issuing this letter to provide an overview of a school district's responsibilities under the Individuals with Disabilities Education Act (IDEA) to address bullying of students with disabilities.[1]

As discussed in this letter, and consistent with prior Dear Colleague Letters the Department has published, bullying of a student with a disability that results in the student not receiving meaningful educational benefit constitutes a denial of a free appropriate public education (FAPE) under the IDEA that must be remedied.[2] However, even when situations do not rise to a level that constitutes a denial of FAPE, bullying can undermine a student's ability to achieve his or her full academic potential. Attached to this letter are specific strategies that school districts and schools[3] can implement to effectively prevent and respond to bullying, and resources for obtaining additional information.

Bullying of any student by another student, for any reason, cannot be tolerated in our schools.[4] Bullying is no longer dismissed as an ordinary part of growing up, and every effort should be made to structure environments and provide supports to students and staff so that bullying does not occur. Teachers and adults should respond quickly and consistently to bullying behavior and

---

[1] This letter is intended to supplement the July 25, 2000, joint Dear Colleague Letter from OSERS and the Department's Office for Civil Rights (OCR), which addressed disability harassment under Section 504 of the Rehabilitation Act of 1973 (Section 504), Title II of the Americans with Disabilities Act of 1990 (Title II of the ADA), and the IDEA (available at: http://www.ed.gov/ocr/docs/disabharasssltr.html).

[2] Some bullying of students with disabilities may also constitute discriminatory harassment and trigger additional responsibilities under the civil rights laws that OCR enforces, including Section 504, Title II of the ADA, Title VI of the Civil Rights Act of 1964, and Title IX of the Education Amendments of 1972. See OCR's October 26, 2010, Dear Colleague Letter on Harassment and Bullying (available at: http://www.ed.gov/ocr/letters/colleague-201010.html).

[3] In the context of this letter "school" includes public preschools; elementary, middle, and high schools; and public agencies, including the State Educational Agency (SEA), Educational Service Agencies (ESA), Local Educational Agencies (LEA), nonprofit public charter schools that are not otherwise included as LEAs or ESAs and are not a school of an LEA or ESA, and any other political subdivisions of the State that are responsible for providing education to children with disabilities. See 34 C.F.R. §300.33.

[4] Although the focus of this letter is peer-to-peer bullying, it is important to acknowledge that it is also intolerable for teachers and school staff to be party to school bullying and disability harassment (*i.e.,* being active participants in bullying), or observers to school bullying without taking action to address the behavior. While teacher-student disability harassment also may constitute a denial of FAPE, those issues are beyond the scope of this letter. We recommend that States and school districts consult with legal counsel regarding their responsibilities and duties in cases of bullying that involve school personnel, including taking the matter seriously, and promptly addressing any problematic behaviors.

send a message that bullying is not acceptable. Intervening immediately to stop bullying on the spot can help ensure a safer school environment.

Bullying is characterized by aggression used within a relationship where the aggressor(s) has more real or perceived power than the target, and the aggression is repeated, or has the potential to be repeated, over time. Bullying can involve overt physical behavior or verbal, emotional, or social behaviors (e.g., excluding someone from social activities, making threats, withdrawing attention, destroying someone's reputation) and can range from blatant aggression to far more subtle and covert behaviors. Cyberbullying, or bullying through electronic technology (e.g., cell phones, computers, online/social media), can include offensive text messages or e-mails, rumors or embarrassing photos posted on social networking sites, or fake online profiles.

Addressing and reporting bullying is critical. Students who are targets of bullying behavior are more likely to experience lower academic achievement and aspirations, higher truancy rates, feelings of alienation from school, poor relationships with peers, loneliness, or depression.[5] Bystanders, or those who only see or hear about bullying, also may be negatively affected as bullying tends to have harmful effects on overall school climate. Bullying can foster fear and disrespect and negatively affect the school experience, norms, and relationships of all students, families, and school personnel.[6] The consequences may result in students changing their patterns of school participation or schools eliminating school activities (e.g., dances, sporting events) where bullying has occurred. Teachers, school personnel, parents, and students should report bullying when they become aware of it.

Students with disabilities are disproportionately affected by bullying.[7] For example, students with learning disabilities, attention deficit or hyperactivity disorder, and autism are more likely to be bullied than their peers.[8] Any number of factors -- physical characteristics, processing and social skills, or intolerant environments -- may increase the risk that students with disabilities will be bullied. Due to the characteristics of their disabilities, students with intellectual, communication, processing, or emotional disabilities may not understand the extent to which bullying behaviors are harmful, or may be unable to make the situation known to an adult who can help. In circumstances involving a student who has not previously been identified as a child with a disability under the IDEA, bullying may also trigger a school's child find obligations under the IDEA. 34 C.F.R. §§300.111, 300.201.

Whether or not the bullying is related to the student's disability, any bullying of a student with a disability that results in the student not receiving meaningful educational benefit constitutes a

---

[5] Gini G., & Pozzoli T. (2009). Association between bullying and psychosomatic problems: A meta-analysis. *Pediatrics,*123(3):1059-1065.

[6] O'Brennan, L. M., Bradshaw, C. P., & Sawyer, A. L. (2009). Examining developmental differences in the social-emotional problems among frequent bullies, victim, and bully/victims. Psychology in the Schools, 46(2), 100-115.

[7] Swearer, S. M., Wang, C., Maag, J. M., Siebecker, A., B., & Frerichs, L. J. (2012). Understanding the bullying dynamic among students in special and general education. *Journal of School Psychology, 50,* 503-520.

[8] Twyman, K. A., Saylor, C. F., Saia, D., Macias, M. M., Taylor, L. A., & Spratt, E. (2010). Bullying and ostracism experiences in children with special health care needs. *Journal of Developmental Behavioral Pediatrics, 31,* 1-8.

denial of FAPE under the IDEA that must be remedied.[9] States and school districts have a responsibility under the IDEA, 20 U.S.C. § 1400, *et seq.*, to ensure that FAPE in the least restrictive environment (LRE) is made available to eligible students with disabilities. In order for a student to receive FAPE, the student's individualized education program (IEP) must be reasonably calculated to provide meaningful educational benefit.[10]

Schools have an obligation to ensure that a student with a disability who is the target of bullying behavior continues to receive FAPE in accordance with his or her IEP. The school should, as part of its appropriate response to the bullying, convene the IEP Team to determine whether, as a result of the effects of the bullying, the student's needs have changed such that the IEP is no longer designed to provide meaningful educational benefit. If the IEP is no longer designed to provide a meaningful educational benefit to the student, the IEP Team must then determine to what extent additional or different special education or related services are needed to address the student's individual needs; and revise the IEP accordingly. Additionally, parents have the right to request an IEP Team meeting at any time, and public agencies generally must grant a parental request for an IEP Team meeting where a student's needs may have changed as a result of bullying. The IDEA placement team (usually the same as the IEP Team) should exercise caution when considering a change in the placement or the location of services provided to the student with a disability who was the target of the bullying behavior and should keep the student in the original placement unless the student can no longer receive FAPE in the current LRE placement. While it may be appropriate to consider whether to change the placement of the child who was the target of the bullying behavior, placement teams should be aware that certain changes to the education program of a student with a disability (*e.g.,* placement in a more restrictive "protected" setting to avoid bullying behavior) may constitute a denial of the IDEA's requirement that the school provide FAPE in the LRE. Moreover, schools may not attempt to resolve the bullying situation by unilaterally changing the frequency, duration, intensity, placement, or location of the student's special education and related services. These decisions must be made by the IEP Team and consistent with the IDEA provisions that address parental participation.

If the student who engaged in the bullying behavior is a student with a disability, the IEP Team should review the student's IEP to determine if additional supports and services are needed to address the inappropriate behavior. In addition, the IEP Team and other school personnel should consider examining the environment in which the bullying occurred to determine if changes to the environment are warranted.

As discussed above, any bullying of a student with a disability that results in the student not receiving meaningful educational benefit from the special education and related services provided by the school is a denial of FAPE. A student must feel safe in school in order to fulfill his or her full academic potential. We encourage States and school districts to alert Boards of Education, school administrators, teachers, and staff that bullying can result in a denial of FAPE

---

[9] OCR also has authority to investigate complaints alleging denial of FAPE under Section 504 and Title II. See the July 25, 2000, joint Dear Colleague Letter on Disability Harassment; (available at: http://www.ed.gov/ocr/docs/disabharassltr.html); and OCR's October 26, 2010, Dear Colleague Letter on Harassment and Bullying (available at: http://www.ed.gov/ocr/letters/colleague-201010.html).

[10] See *Hendrick Hudson Central Sch. Dist. Bd. of Educ. v. Rowley*, 458 U.S. 176, 201 (1982).

for students with disabilities. We also encourage States and school districts to reevaluate their policies and practices addressing problematic behaviors, including bullying, in light of the information provided in this letter, as well as in OSERS' July 25, 2000, joint Dear Colleague Letter and OCR's October 26, 2010, Dear Colleague Letter. The enclosure to this letter, "Effective Evidence-based Practices for Preventing and Addressing Bullying," includes practices for use as part of any bullying prevention and intervention program to help ensure that school and classroom settings are positive, safe, and nurturing environments for all children and adults.

We look forward to continuing to work with you to ensure that students with disabilities have access to high-quality services in positive, safe, and respectful school environments.

Sincerely,

Melody Musgrove, Ed. D.
Director
Office of Special Education Programs

Michael K. Yudin
Acting Assistant Secretary

Enclosure: Effective Evidence-based Practices for
                     Preventing and Addressing Bullying

SERVICE ANIMALS UNDER THE AMERICANS WITH DISABILITIES ACT (ADA)

Service Animals under the ADA

On September 15, 2010, the Department of Justice published revised final regulations implementing the ADA for Title II (state and local government services) and Title III (public accommodations and commercial facilities). The revised regulations contain a number of provisions which relate to service animals in schools. The following is a brief overview and summary of service animals under the ADA.

What is a "Service Animal" under the ADA?

A service animal is defined as "any dog that is individually trained to do work or perform tasks for the benefit of an individual with a disability." 28 C.F.R. § 35.104. Therefore, any animal that is not a "dog" cannot be a service animal under the ADA.[3] Under the ADA, a "service animal" does not include a dog that is not yet trained or still in training. This means that a "service animal" in training does not meet the federal definition of a service animal and does not need to be treated as one. State law, however, may require a different standard. In Minnesota, for example, a service dog in training is allowed to be in any public place. Minn. Stat. § 256C.02.

How may a School Determine Whether an Animal Qualifies as a "Service Animal"?

A public entity (such as a school) may only make two inquiries to determine whether an animal qualifies as a "service animal." They are: (1) is the animal required because of a disability; and (2) what work or task has the animal been trained to perform? 28 C.F.R. § 35.136(f). This means that a school may not ask questions about a dog's particular training or licensing when determining whether it qualifies as a "service animal" or not. A school, however, may exclude an animal if it determines it is not a "service animal" based upon these two questions. For example, if the animal is not required because of a disability, it is not a service animal. Likewise, if the dog's work or task

---

[3] A school must also make reasonable modifications to accommodate a miniature horse that has been individually trained to do or perform tasks for people with disabilities. 28 U.S.C. § 35.136(i).

is not directly related to the disability, or the dog is not proficient in the task or work, it may not qualify as a "service animal" under the ADA. A school needs to be careful when determining if a dog is not a "service animal," and needs to be prepared to answer: (1) who made the determination; and (2) what specific facts did the person rely upon when making the determination. Since the ADA gives an individual with a disability a "right" to a "service animal," careful consideration needs to be given when determining a dog does not qualify as a "service animal."

Can You Exclude a "Service Animal"?

Once it has been determined that a dog properly qualifies as a "service animal," it may only be removed from the premise under two conditions. First, a "service animal" may be removed if the animal is out of control, and the animal's handler does not take effective action to control it. 28 C.F.R. § 35.136(b). Second, a "service animal" may be removed if the animal is not housebroken. *Id.* Absent these two situations, the service animal must be allowed. A child may be the dog's handler, but must maintain control over the animal via the use of a harness, a leash, or by other effective means if the harness or leash would interfere with the performance of the service animal's work or tasks. C.F.R. § 35.136(d). If a child cannot handle the dog, the parents would typically have to provide a handler.[4] A school, however, is not responsible for the care and supervision of a service animal. C.F.R. § 35.136(e).

---

[4] Although a school is typically not required to provide any assistance in handling a service animal under the ADA, a recent case found that minimal assistance of tethering and untethering a "service animal" for a child handler is required when the child could otherwise maintain control of the animal. *Gate-Chili Cen. School Dist.*, 65 IDELR 152 (DOJ 2015). Also, if the animal is needed to provide a FAPE, the school may have to provide additional assistance (discussed later). Otherwise, the school is not required to provide any handling assistance.

Service Animals under Section 504/IDEA

The revised regulations from the Department of Justice, published on September 15, 2010, contain a number of provisions which relate to "service animals" in schools. These regulations, however, do not apply to "service animals" as a "related service" under the IDEA and Section 504. *See* Letter from U.S. Dept. of Housing and Urban Development (Feb. 17, 2011).

A student's access to a service animal under Section 504 is essentially the second step in a two-step process. The first step is to apply the ADA, and if the dog qualifies as service animal, the student is permitted to have the dog in school. Even if an animal does not meet the ADA definition of a "service animal," Section 504 must still be analyzed to see if the animal would be permitted or required in order to provide the student with a FAPE.

Section 504 and the IDEA require a school to provide "related services" for a person with disabilities in order to provide a FAPE. *See* 20 U.S.C. §§ 1401(26) and 1412. The IEP or 504 team must consider what special education and "related services" are necessary for FAPE. A related service could include the use of a service animal.

The 504 or IDEA team would consider a parent's request for a service animal or a therapy animal as a "related service" designed to enable the student with disabilities to receive a FAPE. For example, the team might consider whether a pet rabbit or parrot that calms the student when she is anxious is a "related service." If the student's anxiety can be managed in other ways, the team could certainly choose other appropriate services and exclude the animal, as long as the student still receives a FAPE.

In summary, under the ADA, if the dog qualifies as a service animal, the student is entitled to have the dog at school. In some rare cases, a parent or guardian may request that a service animal or therapy animal be a part of the 504 Plan or the IEP. The team must consider whether the student requires the animal in order to receive a FAPE. If other means are available, the team may agree upon other means to support the student.

Administrative Guidance – Case Summaries

Bakersfield City Sch. Dist., 50 IDELR 169 (OCR 2008).

"Consider ADA, then consider FAPE"

Facts: A student with autism brought a dog as a "service animal" to assist with the student's behavior. The district eventually determined the dog was not a "service animal" under the ADA and prohibited its use on school grounds.

Holding: The district must follow all procedural requirements when determining whether or not a dog qualifies as a "service animal" under the ADA, and if it is determined the dog is not a service animal, the district still needs to do an analysis of whether the dog is necessary for the student to receive a FAPE.

Trinity Area Sch. Dist., 56 IDELR 143 (OCR 2010).

"Always have the discussion"

Facts: A student with autism was denied the use of a dog that helped manage the child's behavior. The dog was trained to give deep pressure therapy. The district asserted that the dog was a "comfort animal," and its functions were addressed adequately by the student's IEP. The district did meet to discuss the use of the dog at an IEP meeting, but the "discussion" only included the parents' requests and the district's denial for the parents, failing to give sufficient information about the dog.

Holding: The district did not follow the Section 504 procedural safeguards/regulations when it did not sufficiently consider the dog's impact on the student's safety, adaptive behavior, and ability to meet social and behavioral goals. The district needed to actually deliberate about whether the dog was an appropriate and required element to provide the student a FAPE.

Takeaway: Always have the discussion. Discuss a proposed use of an animal for providing FAPE even if its use is unlikely because the school already provides a proper alternative means to provide the student a FAPE.

<u>Gates-Chili Cen. Sch. Dist., 65 IDELR 152 (DOJ 2015).</u>

"Separation of ADA and FAPE"

Facts: A young, nonverbal student with several disabilities (Angelman Syndrome, autism, epilepsy, asthma and hypotonia), had a service animal for use in school. There was no dispute that the dog was individually trained to perform tasks for the benefit of the student and met the definition of a service animal under the ADA. The school told the parent that it would not allow its staff to assist the child in handling the service dog, and it would not allow the dog in school unless there was an adult handler (either the parent or another person) due to the student's age and inability to vocalize commands to the dog. The parent, therefore, hired a "handler" to accompany the service dog to school during the day at a cost of about $1,400 per month. Although the student could not speak, the student found nonverbal ways to issue the appropriate commands to the service dog and used assistive technology to issue commands to the dog so it could perform its tasks. The parent then requested the student's one-on-one aide to assist in issuing some of the commands and tethering/untethering the animal. The district refused, citing its school policy for service animals.

Under the ADA, a school must make reasonable modifications to its policies, practices or procedures when necessary to avoid discrimination, unless the school can demonstrate that doing so would fundamentally alter the nature of the service, program, or activity. 28 C.F.R. § 31.130(b)(7). Additionally, a school shall modify its policies, practice or procedures to permit the use of a service animal by an individual with a disability. 28 C.F.R. § 31.136(a). The only situations where a school may exclude a service animal is when the dog is out of control and the handler does not take effective control over it, and when the dog is not housebroken. 28 C.F.R. § 35.136(c). A school is not responsible for the care or supervision of a service animal. 28 C.F.R. § 35.136(e).

Holding: The school violated the ADA when it denied the requested assistance, because allowing the aide to help issue commands and tether/untether the animal did not fundamentally alter the nature of the school's policy. The DOJ found that the limited scope of the tasks requested were reasonable and required "minimal" effort. In addition, the DOJ noted that "care and supervision" is distinct from "handling," so the federal regulation did not permit the school's exclusion of the service dog.

Note about FAPE: The DOJ noted that its decision did not address the provision of FAPE. It stated, "whether or not the IDEA's requirements have been met does not determine whether a valid ADA claim would exist." In other words, even if the animal is permitted or denied based on the ADA's definition of a "service animal," the IEP or 504 team should still consider whether the animal is necessary for a FAPE.

Q&A: Service Animals

On September 15, 2010, the Department of Justice published the revised final regulations implementing the ADA for Title II (State and local government services) and Title III (public accommodations and commercial facilities). The revised regulations contain a number of provisions which relate to service animals in schools.

Here are some frequently asked questions developed from the 2010 Department of Justice ("DOJ") webinar on the subject:

1. The parents of a child with autism ask the school to allow the child to have access to his pet rabbit in the afternoons. Afternoons tend to be an especially stressful time of day for the child and stroking the rabbit assists the student to de-escalate. Does the school have to allow the student to have his pet rabbit at school each afternoon?

    A. **No**. The term "service animal" is defined to include dogs only. In years past the Department of Justice saw cases where a variety of animals were claimed to be service animals for disabled individuals, including rabbits, boa constrictors, llamas, etc. The Department of Justice's final rule defines "service animal" as "any dog that is individually trained to do work or perform tasks for the benefit of an individual with a disability." 28 C.F.R. § 35 App. A.

Note: In addition to the provisions about service dogs, the Department's revised ADA regulations have a new, separate provision about miniature horses that have been individually trained to do work or perform tasks for people with disabilities. 28 U.S.C. § 35.136(i).

2. A parent tells the school that the family's dog is in the process of being trained as a service animal and wants her child to begin bringing the dog to school this week. Training will not be completed for about 6 to 8 weeks. Does the school have to allow the student to bring the dog to school at this time?

    A. **No.** "Service animal" does not include those dogs not yet trained or still in training. The animal must be already trained for the ADA to apply. However, under Minnesota state law, any person training a service dog is allowed in public places; therefore, the service dog in training should be allowed in the public places of the school. Minn. Stat. § 256C.02.

3. Because parent believes his disabled child is bullied at school, parent requests that the child be allowed to bring his dog and argues that this is allowed because a service animal may be used under the ADA to provide "minimal protection." Does the school have to allow the student to bring his dog?

    > *Crime deterrence is not "work or tasks" for the purpose of the definition of a "service animal."*

    A. **No.** The ADA regulations were revised to eliminate the "minimal protection" language from the service animal definition for two reasons: (1) the phrase can be interpreted to allow any dog that is trained to be aggressive to qualify as a service animal simply by pairing the animal with a person with a disability; and (2) the phrase can be interpreted to allow any untrained pet dog to qualify as a service animal, since many consider the mere presence of a dog to be a crime deterrent, and thus sufficient to meet the minimal protection standard. The new regulations modify the "minimal protection" language to read "non-violent protection," thereby excluding dogs with traditional "protection training" as service animals and clarifying that the mere crime or aggression -deterrent effect of a dog's presence, by itself, does not qualify as work or tasks for purposes of the service animal definition. 28 C.F.R. § 35 App. A.

4. The dog purposed to be used by a student is the family's dog and was not trained as a service animal by a professional trainer or organization. Can the school deny the dog access on that basis?

   A. **No.** While the regulations require that the dog be "individually trained" to do work or perform tasks for the disabled child, that training need not be conducted by a professional trainer.

5. How many tasks must the dog be individually trained to perform for the child, is one or two enough?

   A. **Yes.** There is no set number or quantity of tasks required. The dog could be trained to perform only one or two tasks for the child; what matters is whether the dog was individually trained to do that work or perform that task for the child.

6. The parent of child with autism wants the student to have the dog at school to provide emotional support. The parent insists that without this emotional support it will be impossible for the child to remain attentive and calm enough to make progress and receive FAPE. The school believes it can provide FAPE without the dog. Does the child get to bring the dog?

   A. **No**, at least not under the ADA. The Department of Justice has clarified that "to do work or perform a task" a dog must be individually trained to do more than simply provide emotional support, provide comfort or provide companionship. Providing emotional support, comfort, and companionship do not constitute "work or tasks" for purposes of the ADA.

   The work or tasks performed by a service animal must be directly related to the individual's disability. Examples of work or tasks include, but are not limited to, assisting individuals who are blind or have low vision with navigation and other tasks, alerting individuals who are deaf or hard of hearing to the presence of people or sounds, providing non-violent protection or rescue work, pulling a wheelchair, assisting an individual during a seizure, alerting individuals to the presence of allergens, retrieving items such as medicine or the telephone, providing physical support and assistance with balance and stability to individuals with mobility disabilities, and helping persons with psychiatric and neurological disabilities by preventing or interrupting impulsive or destructive behaviors. The crime deterrent effects of an animal's presence and the provision of emotional support, well-being, comfort, or companionship do not constitute work or tasks for the purposes of this definition. 28 C.F.R. § 35 App. A.

7. Are the following examples of "work" or "tasks" under the ADA?

   A. A child with autism bolts when upset. The dog is trained to immediately resist the bolting by putting pressure on the leash. (**Yes**)

   B. A child with autism sometimes flails about on the floor, the dog is trained to lay on top of the child to apply pressure and stop the flailing. (**Yes**)

> *Students have a right to a service animal even if an aide could perform the task better.*

8. Given the examples in #7, school staff assert that they have techniques to use when the child bolts or flails, and staff insists that their techniques are better than what the dog can do. Does the child get to bring the dog?

   A. **Yes. According to the DOJ, even if a person/aide can perform the task better than the animal, the disabled child has a right to the dog.** The question is whether the dog is individually trained to do work or perform tasks for the child with a disability. If so, the child has a right to the animal under the ADA.

9. A Parent says that his child needs the dog at school because it has an innate ability to calm his child. Does the student get the dog?

   A. **No. The key here is again whether the dog has been individually trained to do work or perform tasks for the child.** Because every dog can calm someone, the animal has to do more than what's innate; it has to be trained individually for a specific task. For example, if a dog is trained to react to a child's impending or increasing aggressiveness by immediately moving closer and brushing up against the child or putting pressure on the child, that would qualify.

10. What right does the school have if it believes a dog is not proficient at the task?

   A. **According to DOJ staff, the school always has the right to challenge whether the dog is, in fact, a trained service animal.**

> *Be very cautious when challenging whether a dog qualifies as a "service animal."*

   However, according to DOJ staff, schools should take care when doing so. When addressing a complaint brought by a parent in this situation, the DOJ will make a careful analysis of how the school arrived at its determination that the dog was not a trained service animal. Schools will need to be prepared to answer: (1) who made the determination; and (2) what specific facts that individual relied upon when making that determination.

11. Can a school ask if a dog has a license?

   A. **No**. A public entity may only make two inquiries to determine whether an animal qualifies as a service animal: (1) is the animal required because of a disability; and (2) what work or task has the animal been trained to perform? 28 C.F.R. § 35.136(f); *see* *also* 28 C.F.R. § 35.136 which allows a public entity to ask an individual with a disability to remove a service animal from the premises if: (1) the animal is out of control and the animal's handler does not take effective action to control it; or (2) the animal is not housebroken.

12. Can a school ask a family to have insurance or ask if they have insurance in case the dog bites someone?

    A. According to DOJ staff, **no**. Again, the DOJ considers these to be impermissible requests because they do not go to the two conditions upon which a public entity may exclude a service animal.

13. Can a school ask whether the dog is housebroken?

    A. According to the DOJ, **no**. The DOJ will strictly construe the rule and considers only two questions permissible: When it is not obvious what service an animal provides; only limited inquiries are allowed. Staff may ask two questions: (1) is the dog a service animal required because of a disability, and (2) what work or task has the dog been trained to perform. Staff cannot ask about the person's disability, require medical documentation, require a special identification card or training documentation for the dog, or ask that the dog demonstrate its ability to perform the work or task. *Guidance on Revised ADA Requirements: Service Animals U.S. Dept. of Justice, July 12, 2011; see* 28 C.F.R. § 35.136(f).

14. Can a school define "housebroken" to include: clean, well-groomed, doesn't steal food from other kids?

    A. **No, according to DOJ staff, schools cannot ask this question or define "housebroken."** DOJ staff note that the issue of food handling would go to whether the dog is under control of the handler which may allow for exclusion.

15. Without asking questions of the family, could a school have a policy on what it means for an animal to be under the handler's control?

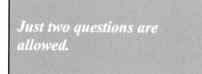
Just two questions are allowed.

    A. According to DOJ staff, schools are only allowed to ask the two questions and are **not allowed** to impose other conditions through policies or requirements that families sign some sort of notice or agreement.

16. Can a school require a handler to undergo a criminal background check?

    A. **Yes, according to DOJ staff if the school requires all school volunteers to have a criminal background check**, then the school can require handlers to undergo a background check. This would be a non-discriminatory action because it is required of all school volunteers, not just handlers for disabled children's animals.

17. Would the school ever be required to pay for a handler?

    A. Under the **ADA, no**. Under **504 and the IDEA, only if** it is required for FAPE/on the IEP.

18. Can the school tell a family they must use "our handler," e.g., a school staff person, rather than the parent or some other handler preferred by the family?

    A. According to DOJ staff, **no**. It is the DOJ's position that this would be impermissible discrimination. If the dog meets the definition of "service animal," is housebroken and under the control of a handler, then the disabled person has the right to choose who will do the handling.

19. Can the school require the parent to handle the dog if the child cannot do it his/herself?

    A. According to DOJ staff, **yes**. If the child is not able to handle the dog, the family must provide the handler. The school is not required to provide the handler. Minimal assistance (such as tethering and untethering the dog); however, may be required if the child may otherwise handle the dog themselves. *See Gates-Chili Cen. Sch. Dist.*, 65 IDELR 152 (DOJ 2015).

20. Does school staff have to take the dog to the bathroom?

    A. **No**, but school staff may have to accompany the child when the child takes the dog to the bathroom. This would constitute a reasonable accommodation for the child.

21. Would a service animal ever be a "fundamental alteration" of the school's program?

    A. According to DOJ staff, they would be hard-pressed to think of a set of circumstances where this would be the case.

22. What should a school do in the case of competing interests where one family wants their child to have a service animal and another family objects because their child is severely allergic to pet dander?

> *Students with allergies to dogs must also be accommodated.*

    A. **It depends**. This type of situation tends to be extremely fact-specific and it is hard to make a blanket statement. According to DOJ staff, the Department will look at the school's analysis of the situation and take into consideration the complicating factors. The Department will look to see whether school officials made a good faith effort to resolve the dilemma through a reasoned analysis considering all the relevant factors. *See West Gilbert Charter Elementary Sch., Inc.*, OCR Case No.: 08-14-1282 (OCR 2015).

Allergies and fear of dogs are not valid reasons for denying access or refusing service to people using service animals. When a person who is allergic to dog dander and a person who uses a service animal must spend time in the same room or facility, for example, in a school classroom or at a homeless shelter, they both should be accommodated by assigning them, if possible, to different locations within the room or different rooms in the facility. Guidance on Revised ADA Requirements: Service Animals U.S. Dept. of Justice, July 12, 2011.

EMPLOYMENT AND THE ADA

Section 504 prohibits discrimination against disabled individuals in: (1) any federal program or activity; and (2) any program or activity receiving federal funds. An individual is considered disabled under Section 504 if he or she meets four requisites: (1) the individual has a disability; (2) the individual is otherwise qualified to participate in the program or activity; (3) the individual was excluded solely by reason of disability; and (4) the program or employer receives federal assistance.

The Americans with Disabilities Act has the same definition of disability as Section 504,[5] but the ADA's coverage is broader. The ADA applies to all employers with 15 or more employees. Additionally, the Minnesota Human Rights Act ("MHRA") applies to any employer regardless of the number of employees. The ADA makes it unlawful to discriminate in all employment practices such as:

---

[5] *See supra*, "Overview of Section 504 of the Rehabilitation Act of 1973 and Related Statutes" for the full definition of an individual with a disability.

In addition, the ADA prohibits retaliation against non-disabled persons who oppose unlawful discrimination against a disabled individual. The ADA prohibits discrimination against those who associate with or provide care to individuals with disabilities. Specifically, an employer may not exclude or deny equal jobs or benefits to, or otherwise discriminate against, a qualified individual because of the known disability of an individual with whom the qualified individual is known to have a family, business, social or other relationship or association. Other forms of employment discrimination include: (1) limiting, segregating or classifying jobs or applicants by disability; (2) contractual discrimination (e.g. health care coverage); (3) pre-employment testing or screening devices for people with disabilities; and (4) pre-employment medical testing as a condition of a job offer, unless it is an essential part of the job.

ADA Requirements for Employers

Employers must provide or at least investigate "reasonable accommodations" for a qualified person with a disability who is able to perform the essential functions of the job. In developing an accommodation, an employer must engage in an "interactive process" with the employee. The interactive process includes: (1) determining the purpose and essential functions of the job; (2) working with the employees to identify barriers to the employee's performance of the essential job function; (3) identifying a range of possible accommodations; and (4) considering whether the accommodation will result in undue hardship to the employer. See the chart below for a list of possible reasonable accommodations.

Undue Hardship

An employer does not have to provide an accommodation if the cost of the accommodation would create an undue financial hardship on the employer. Whether or not an accommodation creates an undue hardship depends on the specific facts of each case. Courts generally look at the nature and the cost of the accommodation and the financial resources of the employer. Creating a new position or hiring a personal helper are not reasonable accommodations and therefore are not required by the ADA. Additionally, tolerating poor performance unrelated to a disability is not a reasonable accommodation.

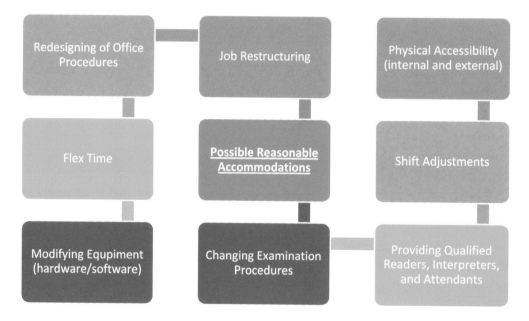

ADA Remedies

Employment cases under the ADA are first investigated by the U.S. Equal Opportunity Employment Commission ("EEOC"). Depending on the result of the investigation, the case may proceed to a jury trial. If a plaintiff wins an ADA cases, the Court is authorized to award compensatory and punitive damages (with some limits depending on the size of the employer). Additionally, the Court may award attorney fees, costs and expert fees. 28 C.F.R. § 36.504.

Q&A: Employment, the ADA, and Section 504

1. Are private schools covered by the Americans with Disabilities Act?

   A. **Probably.** Employers with 15 or more employees are covered by the ADA. Employers who receive federal financial assistance are covered by Section 504. It is possible to be covered by both the ADA and Section 504, one of the statutes, or neither statute.

   > *Employers with 15 or more employees are subject to the Americans with Disabilities Act. Employees who receive federal financial assistance are subject to Section 504.*

2. Do I have to provide a reasonable accommodation that would cost a lot of money?

   A. **It depends.** Employers are required to provide reasonable accommodations for qualified individuals with disabilities. However, an employer is not required to provide an accommodation that would result in an undue hardship to the employer. In determining whether there is an undue hardship, courts look at the nature and cost of the accommodation and the financial resources of the employer.

3. Do I have to create a new job for an individual with a disability?

   A. **No.** Creating an entirely new position is not considered a reasonable accommodation under the ADA.

   > *Employers and employees must engage in an "interactive process" to develop and assess reasonable accommodations for a qualified individual with a disability.*

4. If the employee requests one accommodation, and the employer suggests a different accommodation, which accommodation must the employer provide?

   A. **It depends.** The employer must engage in an interactive process with the employee to develop and assess a reasonable accommodation.

CASE LAW UPDATE

Fry v. Napoleon Cmty. Schs., 137 S.Ct. 743 (2017).
Supreme Court Decision

Issue: Plaintiffs could not recover damages as a remedy under the Individuals with Disabilities Education Act ("IDEA"), but plaintiffs could recover damages as a remedy under the Rehabilitation Act ("Section 504") and the Americans with Disabilities Act ("ADA"). The issue before the Supreme Court was whether a plaintiff must exhaust the IDEA procedural requirements when he or she brings a suit for damages under Section 504 and/or the ADA.

> *If the gravamen of a plaintiff's suit is not related to the IDEA's guarantee of a FAPE, then the plaintiff is not required to exhaust the IDEA's administrative requirements, and the plaintiff can bring suit directly in federal court.*

Held: A plaintiff does not need to exhaust the IDEA's administrative requirements where "the gravamen of the plaintiff's suit is something other than the denial of the IDEA's core guarantee of a FAPE." In other words, IDEA's exhaustion requirements only apply to cases where a plaintiff alleges a denial of a FAPE.

Endrew F. v. Douglas Cnty. Sch. Dist. RE-1, 137 S.Ct. 988 (2017).
Supreme Court Decision

Issue: 35 years ago, the Supreme Court held that the IDEA contained minimum substantive protections for students with disabilities. *Board of Educ. v. Rowley*, 458 U.S. 176 (1982). Under the IDEA, the Court held, schools must provide "individual services sufficient to provide every eligible child with *some* educational benefit." *Id*. The Tenth Circuit Court of Appeals interpreted the Supreme Court's use of "some benefit" in *Rowley* as meaning "more than *de minimis*."

> *In order to meet its substantive obligations for providing a FAPE under the IDEA, a school must offer an IEP reasonably calculated to enable a child to make progress appropriate in light of the child's circumstances.*

Held: A school district has a substantive obligation to provide a disabled student with a FAPE under the Individuals with Disabilities Education Act. In order to meet this obligation, "a school must offer an IEP reasonably calculated to enable a child to make progress appropriate in light of the child's circumstances."

Barnwell v. Watson, 880 F.3d 998 (8th Cir. 2018).
Court of Appeals for the 8th Circuit Decision

Background information: Chandler Barnwell—who was diagnosed with Attention Deficit Hyperactivity Disorder, Depression and Anxiety, Oppositional Defiant Disorder, and Asperger's Disorder—took his own life at the age of 16. It is believed by Chandler's parents that he was a victim of bullying, which pushed him to commit suicide.

From grade school to 9th grade, Chandler attended five different schools. The incident that is believed to have caused his death took place at Parkview Arts Science Magnet High School. Chandler started 9th grade at Parkview Arts Science Magnet High School in August 2010. While attending school, Chandler expressed to his adult peers that he wanted to graduate early or take his GED to leave the school, but he never specifically stated he wanted to leave because of being bullied.

Moreover, the incident that may have caused him to commit suicide happened in class on December 7th. While in class, Chandler was harassed by another student and in response to the bully, Chandler made a mean comment to the student. The student responded to Chandler's comment by allegedly stating, "go home and kill yourself." That night, after his parents had left for an appointment, Chandler took his life.

After Chandler took his life, information came out from his fellow classmates that Chandler was bullied constantly while attending Parkview Arts Science Magnet High School. After Chandler's suicide, his parents tried to start an investigation with the Principal, Booth, but Booth denied Chandler was ever bullied at school.

Issue: After Chandler's suicide, the Barnwells, under Section 504 of the Rehabilitation Act, alleged that the school discriminated against Chandler's disability, when it failed to protect him from being bullied at school. The United States District Court for the Eastern District of Arkansas – Little Rock found no evidence that supported the Barnwells' claim. In response, the Barnwells appealed the District Court's decision.

The Barnwells argued that the school's employees did not address the allegations that Chandler was bullied or harassed at school. In addition, Principal Booth did not conduct a sufficient investigation after Chandler's death, did not provide counselors to those grieving, and silenced individuals who wanted to discuss Chandler's suicide.

Held: After the Eighth Circuit reviewed the case, the court affirmed the District Court's decision that there was no evidence that the school officials knew of any incident of Chandler being bullied. However, the school did know about one incident that occurred on October 7th, which the school responded to right away. In addition, the Eighth Circuit disagreed with the Plaintiffs' claim that a school may discriminate against a disabled student in violation of Section 504 after the student's death, by not investigating the alleged harassment that might have happened before he died.

Special Sch. Dist. No. 1, Minneapolis Pub. Schs. v. R.M.M., 861 F.3d 769 (8th Cir. 2017). Court of Appeals for the 8th Circuit Decision

Background information: R.M.M. was a student who lived in the district boundaries of Minneapolis Public Schools, but voluntarily attended a Catholic private school in Minneapolis. Initially, R.M.M. was bussed twice per week from her private school to a nearby public school for special reading and writing sessions. After enrolling in Minneapolis Public Schools for a short time, R.M.M. returned to her private school. After returning to her private school, the private school informed the Parents that it could no longer meet R.M.M.'s educational needs.

The parents then filed a complaint with the Minnesota Department of Education ("MDE") requesting an impartial due process hearing.

Issue: The district filed suit to review the Administrative Law Judge's ("ALJ") decision that R.M.M., a private school student, had the right to a FAPE. In other words, the issue is whether or not "Minnesota State law goes beyond the minimum requirements of IDEA and entitles private school students the right to FAPE." The second issue that the district appealed is whether or not R.M.M as a private school student had the right to an impartial due process hearing.

Held: The Eighth Circuit found that under Minnesota law, private school students do have the right to FAPE. The Eighth Circuit concluded that Minn. Stat. "Section 125A.03 clearly states, the phrase 'special instruction and services' in the state of Education Code means a free appropriate public education provided to an eligible child with disabilities." On the second issue raised on appeal, the Eighth Circuit found that Minnesota law does not exclude private school children when it states "[a] parent . . . is entitled to an impartial due process hearing . . . when a dispute arises over . . . the provision of a free appropriate public education to a child with a disability." Furthermore, the Eighth Circuit concluded that despite attending a private school, R.M.M. and her parents have the right to an impartial due process hearing.

*Booth Law Group represented the district in this matter.

Holzmueller v. Illinois High Sch. Ass'n, 881 F.3d 587 (7th Cir. 2018).
Court of Appeals for the 7th Circuit Decision

Issue: A high school runner with spastic quadriplegia brought an action under § 1983 seeking accommodations for his disability which would allow him to qualify for state high school track finals. Holzmueller (A.H.) was a full member of his high school's track and field team and had never been prevented from participating in practice or at school track meets. The Illinois High School Association (IHSA) previously established events and divisions within various sports for students with disabilities. IHSA did not establish division for runners with disabilities comparable to A.H.'s. A.H.'s primary request was that IHSA establish separate qualifying times for the state championship track meet for individuals with disabilities. As it stood, there was no way for an individual with disabilities to qualify for the state championship without meeting the qualifications of the non-disabled students.

Held: The court reviewed the standard by which it reviews claims under the Rehabilitation act and the ADA. The court, quoting *Washington v. Ind. High Sch. Athletic Ass'n, Inc.*, 181 F.3d 840, 847 (7th Cir. 1999), stated that "disability discrimination under the Rehabilitation Act and the ADA can be established in three different ways: (1) the defendant intentionally acted on the basis of the disability, (2) the defendant refused to provide a reasonable modification, or (3) the defendant's rule disproportionally impacts disabled people." (internal quotations omitted). Accordingly, the court stated that A.H. would have to show that "but for his physical disability, the normal operation of the qualifying times would have allowed him to qualify for the state championship track meet." The court determined that A.H. could not establish that without his disability, he would be amongst the elite runners that qualify for the state championship track meet.

The court next looked to whether IHSA failed to provide A.H. with a reasonable accommodation. Citing *Southeastern Cmty. Coll. v. Davis*, 99 S. Ct. 2361(1979), the court held that "lowering particular eligibility or qualifying requirements established by an entity can be substantial modifications that are unreasonable." The court determined that changing the qualifications for the state championship track meet would "underscore the essence of the sport: one must run as fast as possible to achieve the predetermined times" and was thus unreasonable.

The court concluded that because A.H. had the opportunity to compete and qualify for the state championship track meet, he was provided with the same opportunity as non-disabled student athletes.

Arcadia Unified Sch. Dist., OCR Case No. 09-14-1322 (OCR 2014).
Office of Civil Rights Decision

A school district has discriminated against an individual student where there is:

1. Evidence that the individual was treated differently than non-disabled individuals under similar circumstances;
2. The treatment has resulted in a denial or limitation of services, benefits or opportunities; and
3. The school district cannot provide a nondiscriminatory reason or provide a nondiscriminatory reason that is found to be a pretext for discrimination.

At a middle school in the Arcadia school district, teachers were dismissing students five minutes before the end of the school day. They dismissed the students early because the students needed to use the restroom before a long bus ride home. Teachers asserted that the students were still receiving instruction for these five minutes in the form of social and behavioral skill training. Arcadia was found to have discriminated because:

> *504 students must have the same school day as their peers unless the team finds otherwise based on an individualized determination.*

1. The students in special day classes were receiving five less minutes of instruction than their peers not in special day classes;
2. The students were denied five minutes of valuable classroom time; and
3. The school district dismissed all students five minutes early without making individualized decisions for each student in the special day class and provided no other legitimate reason for early dismissal.

Minneapolis Pub. Schs., OCR No. 05-17-1371 (OCR 2017).
Office of Civil Rights Decision

Section 504 requires that a school district provide parents with notice of procedural safeguards. The procedural safeguards include access to examine relevant records, an impartial hearing with participation for the parents and representation by counsel, and a review procedure. Parents may use these procedural safeguards when they disagree with the identification, evaluation and/or placement of children, or the process used for any of these activities.

In this case, the Complainant asserted that the district did not provide notice of procedural safeguards at a 504 team meeting and did not send the notice via mail or email. In order to prove her claim, the Complainant provided OCR with copies of Student A's revised 504 Plan, but did not provide OCR with signed copies of the procedural safeguards or notice of rights. During the investigation, OCR interviewed Student A's Case Manager, who stated that the procedural safeguards are sent to parents immediately after any Section 504 meeting or whenever a revision is made to a 504 Plan. To investigate further, OCR reviewed the district's copies of Student A's educational records. While reviewing Student A's records, OCR found a copy of the notice of procedural safeguards with the Complainant's signature on it. OCR also found easily accessible information about procedural safeguards on the districts website. Additionally, OCR did not find any proof that the Complainant ever complained to the district that she did not receive notice of her procedural safeguards. Accordingly, the district did not fail to provide notice of procedural safeguards to the Complainant.

Find a simple, efficient way to ensure that parents receive the Notice of Procedural Rights. Document all of your efforts.

Indep. Sch. Dist. No. 279, OCR No. 05-16-1365 (OCR 2016).
Office of Civil Rights Decision

The district received a complaint alleging that it discriminated against Complainant's daughter on the basis of ADHD, in violation of Section 504 and the ADA. Second, Complainant alleged that the district retaliated against Complainant for rejecting services proposed by the district and pressuring Complainant to accept, in violation of Section 504 and the ADA.

Student A, who attended a district middle school, received special education services for ADHD and anxiety. Student A was offered social work minutes and/or mental health case management services to help Student A access the curriculum. The Complainant declined because she did not believe Student A needed mental health services

Student A's performance and attendance at school declined. The school held a conciliation meeting to address Complainant's concerns. The special education coordinator and school principal attended the meeting. Complainant stated that she believed the meeting was an attempt to pressure her to accept mental health case management services. After this meeting, Student A's behavior declined, both at home and at school. Complainant stated she was considering hospitalization for Student A.

Complainant became increasingly concerned with Student A's behavior at home, and told the district she was afraid of what would happen if she had to call the police. After getting parental consent, the Chief of Police attended Student A's IEP team meeting to discuss police response to distressed persons. Complainant believed this was another attempt to pressure her into accepting mental health services. Sometime after this meeting, the school asked the Chief of Police to do a welfare check on Student A because the student had been absent for five days, and the district could not get in contact with Complainant.

OCR found in favor of the district on both the harassment and retaliation charges. First, regarding harassment, OCR found that the alleged "harassing" behaviors, such as preferential seating, calling Student A out of the room for work, breaking up assignments, and questions from the social worker were actually required by Student A's IEP. Second, OCR concluded that the district did not retaliate when it offered mental health case management services or requested welfare check on Student A. Offering service is not an adverse act, something required to show retaliation, and the school had a legitimate concern for Student A so its requested welfare check was not retaliatory.

Caution: The district in this case was very careful about involving the police in a student's special education issues. Be cautious that the well-intentioned intervention may be seen as "criminalizing" a student's behavior.

QUESTIONS AND ANSWERS REGARDING SECTION 504 OF THE REHABILITATION ACT

Questions and Answers Regarding Section 504 of the Rehabilitation Act[6]

<u>Section 1 – Eligibility for a 504 plan</u>

Question 1: Can or should we write a 504 Plan without a diagnosis?

Answer: Best practice is to have the parent/guardian obtain a mental health or medical diagnosis as part of the evaluation process. The law permits the school to request a diagnosis, but does not require a diagnosis. Accordingly, there may be occasions where the team writes a plan without a diagnosis, or where the district pays for an outside diagnosis. THESE SHOULD BE EXTREMELY RARE SITUATIONS-PLEASE SEEK CONSULT FROM YOUR DIRECTOR OR COUNSEL IN THESE CASES.

Q.1 (a): How should the Section 504 team proceed with students who have "perceived" disabilities when no formal diagnosis is available?

Answer: If school staff believes that a student may have a disability and needs a 504 Plan, the staff should propose an evaluation. If the parent/guardian can't or won't obtain a diagnosis, the school staff has to determine if the district needs a formal diagnosis and if so, it must provide one.

Keep in mind that the law uses the word "perceived" to describe a situation where staff treats a child as disabled based on a mistaken belief (or without proper documentation of a disability) that the child has a disability. Only a student with a diagnosed disability whose disability requires program changes at school to avoid discrimination will have a 504 Plan. On rare exceptions, a school may decide to provide a 504 Plan for a student without the documentation – but that is not because the disability is "perceived"- it is because it is a real disability and some barrier has prevented obtaining a diagnosis. We will discuss this more in our in-service.

Q.1 (b): Does a school have to do an evaluation for Section 504 if formally requested by parent?

Answer: No, Section 504 does not require that the district do an evaluation of a student simply because a parent requests it. However, a refusal by the district to do an evaluation is an action with respect to the student's evaluation and placement, and therefore the district must provide the parent with procedural safeguards. The parent must be notified of their right to request a hearing over the decision not to evaluate.

Q.1 (c): What are the requirements of "child find" within section 504? What should happen if there's a medical diagnosis, but no parent request?

Answer: The law requires that a school district must evaluate any child the district has reason to believe may be disabled under Section 504's legal definition. The district's child find obligation

---

[6] These questions were compiled from those submitted by several clients. They are not meant to be an outline of Section 504 but instead, a review of the frequently asked questions and our responses.

is not contingent on parent request. If district staff believes the child may need a 504 Plan, school staff should propose an evaluation. Keep in mind that you need a parent permission to do an initial 504 evaluation.

Q.1 (d): Who can provide the diagnosis? Physician? Therapist/nurse practitioner?

Answer: Any person who is licensed to make a diagnosis can provide one for 504 purposes. This would include an M.D., D.O., psychologist, Licensed Clinical Social Worker, nurse practitioner or any provider who is licensed to make a diagnosis. Also, keep in mind that the 504 Team must consider information from a variety of sources, e.g., teacher reports, tests, etc. Additionally, remember that the 504 team has discretion to weight the information received and can give due weight to the information received depending on: (1) the source of the information; (2) how thorough the information appears to be; and (3) whether the information appears reliable when compared to other information before the team.

Practice Tip: **Always request the diagnosis from the parent. If they can't or won't obtain one, seek advice from your director – don't simply refuse the 504 Plan. We don't want the student to be harmed because of parental inaction or inability.**

Second, accept the diagnosis – if you have questions about the ability of the person to make the diagnosis, seek advice from your director. Not every child with a diagnosis will get a 504 Plan so don't get hung up on this stage.

Q.2: Who is responsible for "assessing" a student's needs? Counselors are not trained diagnosticians, so does this fall to the family to provide medical records?

Answer: The 504 team conducts the assessment. No school staff is required to provide a diagnosis. Instead, the parent/guardian obtains an outside diagnosis AND the school staff considers input from teachers, discipline records, health and attendance records. The staff may also recommend some formal testing such as IQ testing, assessment of academics, etc. Those instruments are generally in school and are administrated by a person trained to do so.

Q.3: If a student/parent wants a 504 Plan, but the student has all A's and is doing well in school, is this something we should proceed with?

Answer: It depends on whether the student is eligible for a plan. In our training, we will discuss a 3 step process for determining eligibility – grades are on important factor, but not the determinative factor. If the school staff decides not to evaluate the student for 504 eligibility, you must provide the parent with the notice of procedural safeguards so they understand their right to request a hearing. Keep in mind that it is not the parent or student's desires that dictate whether the student is eligible or requires a plan. Instead, it is the 504 team that determines eligibility, whether a plan is necessary, and its contents.

Section 2 – Section 504 Team

Q.4: Who should be on the 504 team? Who leads these meetings? Do all meetings have to include all members of the team? If not, who is essential?

Answer: The 504 team should include someone who knows the child and someone who understands the disability and the parent/guardian and child if appropriate for the child. **SECTION 504 DOES NOT REQUIRE MEETINGS.** We would strongly encourage you to meet once if necessary to establish relationship or if the parent requests but do everything from there on via email or mail or phone. Staff doesn't need to meet – use email to "discuss" needs, program changes, and implementation and follow up.

If you do want to meet, have the fewest people present who can describe needs and make a workable plan. Get input via email before the meeting. Of course, if a parent has real concerns re: math and wants the math teacher there, have her available. (She can attend via SKYPE or phone too).

Regarding who should "lead" – even if you don't have a physical meeting, you should have one person responsible for the 504 evaluations and development. If the counselor in your building is responsible for the plans, that person ensures the district's time lines are followed, makes sure that the parent/guardian has notice of their rights, ensures teachers have a plan, and follows up to ensure a plan is implemented and is successful for the student.

Q.5: Does a Nurse have to be present at the team meeting?

Answer: See number 4 above. If you need medical information or interpretation or the nurse is going to provide the program changes (e.g. administer insulin), he or she should be part of the team and have input.

Q.6: Are 30 school days a reasonable amount of time for evaluation? What about 7 school days for a response to initial request?

Answer: Yes, these are reasonable time limits. However, we recommend that you give yourselves a longer time-frame, for example 45 days and 10 days.

Section 3 – Responsibilities

Q.7: Do we need the signatures of teachers or a confirmation they have been notified about a student's 504 Plan? Can we send email notifications and keep a record with dates? What documentation is legally required?

Answer: Our recommendation is that you send the 504 Plan to teachers via email and that you have a date where you follow up via email asking if the 504 Plan is being implemented, grades. The follow up email should also inquire as to the attendance of student, behavior issues or work completion issues, whether the program changes seem to be effective for student and if the teacher has recommendations for changes or modifications.

Q.8: Who is responsible for ensuring teachers are following a 504 Plan? Who enforces if/when teachers do not?

Answer: Each staff person is responsible for implementation of the 504 Plan. It would be a performance issue for the staff person's supervisor to be aware of a teacher or other staff that is not following a 504 Plan. You will want to speak with your director about how your district wants the supervisor to get this information. This is the similar to the responsibilities under the IDEA.

Q.9: If we were to be audited by the OCR or there was a complaint made by a parent, what would the OCR look for? What are the most common findings against schools in cases like this?

Answer: We have reviewed an OCR audit and OCR complaint below.

Audit- The OCR can audit a school's compliance with Section 504. In an audit, the OCR will be looking for:

- A 504 policy
- 504 practices that provide for: child find (identification of disabled students); evaluation; eligibility determinations; and notice to parents of their rights.

The OCR is required to ensure that the district has policies and practices that afford due process. It will be reviewing whether there is such a **process, and that the process was followed.**

Complaint – If there is a complaint by a parent or interested person, the OCR will examine the process that was used and will not "second guess" the determinations of the team. OCR is required by federal regulation to encourage the school to come to a voluntary resolution. This is the case even if the parent/guardian is not in agreement with the resolution.

The most common issues reviewed by OCR are failure to have process for eligibility, failure to evaluate and create a plan in a timely fashion, failure to implement the plan.

Section 4 – Program Changes & 504 Plans

Q. 10: How do we address a situation where parents are seeking specific accommodations (testing in another location or reading tests to students) that we don't have the resources to fulfill?

Answer: The 504 Team, not just the parent/guardian, determine what program changes are needed to prevent discrimination. If the team determines that the appropriate accommodation for a student is testing in another room or reading the test to the student, the district must provide this accommodation. HOWEVER, keep in mind that the district can consider cost and resources and can find other accommodations that are within its resources. For example, the student may take the test at another time when a location is available, may use headphones, may take a test online, or may have another measure of performance to avoid testing, etc.

Q.10 (a): Can we get these types of resources from the district? What if we don't have the funding for these accommodations but they need to be fulfilled?

Answer: Yes, the district has to provide what the student requires. Again, the team (and the school staff in particular) should be looking for program changes that are doable, cost effective and help the student learn self-advocacy and management of her own needs. Cost is rarely a defense – meaning that a court reviewing such a claim will not consider that cost of a paraprofessional to be prohibitive because of the size of the district's budget. As a school professional, you have to consider how the provision of a "rich" program for one student may impact the district's ability to serve all students including those with more significant disabilities and those without identified disabilities.

Q.11: Do we have to write a 504 Plan to accommodate transportation?

Answer: If a student needs a different type of transportation due to a disability, you would write transportation on the 504 Plan. The team should consider and parent/guardian should be advised of their rights under IDEA.

The question you are asking may relate to a temporary issue such as a student who has a broken leg and needs door to door transport for less than six months. In such a case, the law would not require a 504 Plan. It may be district practice to do this for funding reasons – we would have to learn more to provide a district-specific answer. Please speak with your director about this.

Q.12: Is there data available regarding how a need and an accommodation pair together? How do we know if an accommodation is actually helping?

Answer: We are not aware of data or research that supports particular accommodations. However, there is a lot of research regarding how to support certain disabilities such as Asperger's syndrome or dyslexia. Most of that research seems geared toward direct instruction strategies that are often (but not always) part of a 504 Plan.

That being said, the team will design accommodations based on their knowledge of the disability, the needs that are apparent at school or in school activities and the team should have a way of reviewing whether that accommodation is successful. Success can be evaluated by increased performance (attendance, health grades, testing), as well as teacher, parent, and student input.

Q.13: Can we provide accommodations that are not on the "suggested" list in Campus?

Answer: As people are always noting on pins on Pinterest – "yes please!" In fact, since the law requires program changes necessary for an individual student to have access and avoid discrimination, it would be effective to use non-listed program changes when a student requires them.

Q.13 (a): Is it good practice to include separate sections on the 504 Plans for _Student Responsibilities, Parent Responsibilities, and School Responsibilities_? Staff recalls being warned against using these separate sections because "if it is on a 504 Plan, the school is responsible to make sure it happens—if it says "student will" and student does not…we will be held accountable."

Answer: Generally, the Section 504 Plan should stick to listing the accommodations and the settings, or situations in which those accommodations are to be provided. You want to avoid writing plans which require the student or parent to request the accommodation. One exception would be where the student is working on self-advocacy skills. For example, the plan may say:

> "Laura will request a quiet place for testing if she cannot work in general education classroom. The case manage will monitor this accommodation and if Laura is not able to request or does not request a quiet room when necessary, the case manage will ask the teacher to provide one."

Q.13 (b): Is using language in the plan like "student may benefit from" or "teachers may do something" too ambiguous and open to interpretation?

Answer: Yes, this language would generally be too ambiguous. The danger with such language is that staff may be unclear whether/when the accommodation is needed, and the accommodation simply wouldn't be provided. Clear language in the plan will help avoid this.

Q.13 (c): How shall we proceed with 504's and concussions? Are students held accountable for learning when they need brain rest? How do we grade and measure outcomes?

Answer: The 504 team should do an evaluation if the concussive symptoms are expected to last more than six months. This is a developing area of medical and legal issues. Thus, we would recommend that for any student who notifies the school of a concussion, the school should:

- Provide the parent/guardian with notice of 504 & IDEA rights.
- Ask for a medical diagnosis and specifically inquire if the provider estimates that the concussion symptoms will last more than 6 months.

- If the symptoms are to last more than 6 months, write a 504 plan if the student needs it to avoid discrimination.
- If the symptoms are not projected to last more than 6 months, consider an individualized learning plan for the short term.
- 504 grading would be based on the team's determination of what the student needs to learn to earn a grade or credit.

Q.13 (d): Can and should the district pass individual ("PI") 504 students on GRAD tests based on the student and their limitations?

Answer: Based on our discussions with the Office for Civil Rights ("OCR") and the Minnesota Department of Education ("MDE") and our own legal analysis, it is theoretically possible for a student to have a 504 program change for PI on standardized tests. HOWEVER, in most circumstances, if a student's disability prevents them from passing at the state required standard, the student should be considered for an Individual Education Program ("IEP") under the special education law. There may be exceptions to this and they should be identified and discussed as early in the educational career as possible. For example, the team might consider a PI for a student who came to the US for the first time as an 18-year-old, with no prior formal education, no knowledge of English AND a learning disability (that does not meet the criteria for an IEP) is identified by the school. Generally speaking, the student who needs a PI should probably be an IEP student, but again, there may be exceptions.

Q.14: How should we treat 504's and Health Plans?

Answer: A student with a diagnosed medical or mental health disability should have a 504 Plan. Parents need to have notice of their rights under 504.

Q.15: How often should plans be reviewed? How formal is the review? Can this be covered by an informal invitation to parents?

Answer: The Section 504 regulations do not set a time frame. We recommend a review at times of major transition, e.g., elementary school to middle school, middle school to high school, - more frequently if it appears the plan needs adjustment. The review can be done informally, e.g., by email.

Q.16: Does there have to be a notification slip in the cumulative file that there is also a 504 Plan on file? If so, who is responsible for that?

Answer: This would be a district choice. We would recommend that you think less of a cumulative file and more about what is "education data" since most record keeping in the very near future will not involve "files". To your question, it is in the student's and district's best interest for those working with the student including extracurricular and school sponsored event staff to know that the child has a 504 plan.

Q.17: Funding? Do we have financial resources to pay for time, accommodations, and technology?

Answer: Because these program changes are part of general education, there is not separate funding. However, we recommend that school districts think about these costs and establish a budget and project costs. Again, staff has to be concerned with providing what is necessary, but not over-doing the changes so that other students' education suffers.

Q.18: What is the role of a public school with Section 504 in non-public schools?

Answer: The district has child find requirements under Section 504 similar to the IDEA child find obligations. Section 504 requires districts to annually "undertake to identify and locate every qualified [individual with a disability] residing in [the district's] jurisdiction who is not receiving a public education." 34 C.F.R. § 104.2. The 504 regulations do not specify the manner in which school districts must execute their child find duties, and OCR has noted that there are many means available including notices to private schools and local agencies, notices placed in local newspapers, and the like. This notification outreach may be something you want to do in conjunction with the IDEA child find notices that already go out.

One client asked whether the district's counselors who spend time in private schools once a week are required to take the lead on or write 504 Plans for students at the private schools. The costs for counselors to go to the private schools are paid by state dollars. One of the counselors' tasks within your school district is to write 504 plans. We believe that the district's counselors are not required to take the lead on or write 504 plans for students at the private schools. Under Section 504 counseling services are a "related service" and are "those services provided by qualified social workers, psychologists, guidance counselors, or other qualified personnel." 34 C.F.R. § 300.34 (c)(2). Private schools, if they receive federal funds-even indirectly, have their own Section 504 obligations. The district has no obligation to have its counselors writing or taking the lead on writing 504 Plans for students attending private schools.

Q.19: How are early Childhood Family Programs, Community Education and Adult Basic Education ("ABE") connected to Section 504?

Answer: For community education programs and ABE, the district's obligation is the same and each student must be evaluated. The district should provide those accommodations needed to enable the individual to have access to the program or services, and the accommodations must be provided at no cost to the individual. For example, if a child needs adult assistance to be able to be a part of the district's after-care program or a community education program, the district would have to provide that adult assistance and could not condition the child's participation on the grandparent or babysitter accompanying the child to the program. Additionally, the district may not charge more for the child that needs accommodations than the district chargers for non-disabled children. The same would apply to ABE.

A student or child can lawfully be denied access to the program if the child does not meet the requirements such as age or pre-requisite course (for example English 1 before one can participate in English 2). The student can be denied access if even with modifications or accommodations, the student cannot safely participate without fundamentally altering the program. For example, an after school horseback riding program would have to be fundamentally altered if the student, even with a modified saddle or adult assistance, could not safely sit on a horse because of a disability.

Section 5 – IDEA v. 504

Q. 20: Should referral to child study/IDEA precede Section 504 consideration?

Answer: The district may use its child study process before initiating a 504 evaluation, but the child study process must not delay a 504 evaluation when one is necessary. The team should use its best judgment, but must not be overly-tied to the child study process. If it appears that the child needs a 504 evaluation, that evaluation should not be delayed.

The OCR has said that where a school district uses the child study or the Response to Intervention (RTI) process to make determinations about whether a child needs a 504 evaluation, the school district should be giving parents the notice of procedural safeguards and telling them that they have a right to request a 504 evaluation and request a hearing if the parent disagrees with the school district's decision regarding any aspect of the evaluation (including the decision whether to do one, or not). So, for those students in the child study process, particularly those receiving Tier II interventions, you may want to send the parent a notice of procedural safeguards. See Section 6 below.

Q. 21: Is Section 504 an automatic path following exit from special education?

Answer: No. If a student is exited from special education and continues to have medical or mental health diagnosis, the parent or school staff can request a 504 evaluation. If the student is eligible following a 504 evaluation, the 504 Team would write a plan.

Q.22: If the parent rejects an IEP, are we required to provide a 504 plan?

Answer: No. If the parent rejects the IEP, a 504 Plan is not required to be provided. However, there may be exceptions to this rule. Please contact your director if this arises.

Section 6 – RTI and Section 504

Q.23: Is a 504 plan considered a Tier 3 intervention?

Answer: The courts have not looked at the question, and when asked, the OCR has declined to opine on the question of whether interventions provided in RTI are "accommodations" under Section 504.

Our recommendation is that school staff considers RTI interventions to be non-section 504 interventions because they are provided to all general education students who need them regardless of disability status. If, however, the student does not make the expected progress or has other needs, the school should evaluate the student for a 504 Plan. The plan would address any program changes that are needed beyond the RTI interventions.

Q.24: Would there ever be cases where we would formally document Tier 1 Interventions on a 504 Plan? If so, how does it affect our obligation for "child find" if we formally document interventions that are available to all students and expected to adequately support 80% of our students?

Answer: This relates to the last question. Until the courts or OCR weigh in on this, our advice is that if the child is doing well with the Tier 1 interventions, you would not need to do a 504 evaluation and put in place a 504 Plan. This is because the child would not be considered "substantially impaired" as required under Section 504's legal definition of the term "disabled."

Q.24: If a student receiving 504 accommodations is no longer "demonstrating a need" (based on grades/test scores), but continues to have the disability, do we continue to provide them with services? It may be argued that the services are the reason for their success. However, in looking at some 504 Plans, many of the accommodations are part of Tier 1 in the RTI model. If we are looking at continuing eligibility for a student who has ADHD, for example, and the student is showing success from receiving Tier 1 accommodations which are listed on the 504 Plan but are also available to the general population, does the student continue to demonstrate a need for services?

Answer: This question again goes to the issue of whether RTI constitutes an "accommodation." If so, the effect of RTI is to be ignored in determining whether the child is "disabled" under Section 504's legal definition. However, even if the student meets the legal definition of "disabled," you may not need to write a plan because when determining whether the child needs a 504 Plan, you do consider the effects of RTI.

Sample Letter to Parent/Guardian of Student with Medical Needs and Existing Health Plan

[Date]

[Address of Parent(s)/Guardian]

Regarding: Possible Section 504 Qualification

Dear Parent(s) or Guardian:

Your student currently has a health plan that is used at [insert School name]. Your student may be eligible for a Section 504 Plan. Section 504 of the Rehabilitation Act requires schools to provide students with certain program changes that will allow them access to educational opportunities that are similar to their peers. The District is required to give you notice of your rights and the student's rights under this law. The Notice of Section 504 Rights is attached.

In many cases, a Section 504 Plan will contain the same information as the prior health plan. However, in some cases, a 504 Plan may provide other accommodations, modifications or services. A copy of the current health plan is provided. If you would like to meet or have a phone conference to discuss a Section 504 evaluation and whether a Section 504 is required for your student, please contact: _____.

If you would like to discuss the contents of the attached health plan, please contact me as well.

Very Truly Yours,

Enclosures:
Notice of Rights Under Section 504
District's Section 504 Policy